Contents

Part 1

Introduction

Life and works of Samuel Beckett

Samuel Beckett was born into a prosperous middle-class family in Dublin in 1906. He went to a famous Irish public school, Portora Royal, Enniskillen (where Oscar Wilde (1854–1900) had preceded him) and on to Trinity College, Dublin, in 1923. He excelled at sport as well as academic work, touring England with the university cricket team in 1927. As a result of coming first of his year in his modern languages degree, Beckett, in 1928, gained the coveted post of exchange *lecteur* at the École Normale Supérieure in Paris. While there, he is reputed to have puzzled his students by introducing them to the sound of the English language through the music of the German composer Wagner! Beckett amassed, at this time, a large body of notes on the life and work of the philosopher Descartes (1596–1650) with the possibility in mind that they might form the nucleus of a thesis. The thesis never materialised, but the notes formed the basis for the poem 'Whoroscope', which won him the Nancy Cunard prize in 1930.

Beckett described Paris in the twenties as 'a good place for a young man to be'.* The city was at this time the intellectual hub of Europe and humming with new ideas in art and literature. These new ideas can best be categorised under the heading 'Modernism', a general term designating the many remarkable creative experiments that took place in the period between the beginning of the twentieth century and the early thirties. It was a period characterised by great technological change; by the terrifying weapons of the First World War; and by a number of new intellectual theories, such as Sigmund Freud's (1856–1939) writings on psychology, Henri Bergson's (1859–1941) writings on time and Fernand de Saussure's (1857–1913) writings on linguistics. Although it is difficult to give any precise definition to creative eras, most of the major works of Modernism—such as the novels of Marcel Proust (1871–1922) and James Joyce (1882–1941)—attempt to question traditional creative conventions and to find new ways of expressing the complexity of twentieth-century life.

Before he had been long in Paris, Beckett fell under the spell of his fellow Dubliner, James Joyce, one of the most original literary talents of the day. Richard Ellman, in his biography of Joyce, describes the

*John Pilling, *Samuel Beckett*, Routledge, London, 1976, p.3.

two men as engaging 'in conversations which consisted often of silences directed towards each other, both suffused with sadness, Beckett mostly for the world, Joyce mostly for himself'.* In 1929 Beckett's was the first contribution to a book of critical essays on Joyce's 'work in progress' (*Finnegans Wake*, London, 1939), an essay flatteringly entitled 'Dante . . . Bruno. Vico . . Joyce'.**

In 1930 Beckett had to return to Ireland to take up his post as assistant lecturer in the French department at Trinity College. A brilliant academic future seemed assured. But Beckett was hardly more successful with his Irish students than with his French ones. He disliked the confrontation of the classroom, saying, with rare intellectual honesty, that he 'could not bear the absurdity of teaching to others what he did not know himself'.†

Beckett resigned suddenly from the Trinity College post, in the middle of the second year, with the intention of becoming a writer. It is probable that at this stage he considered himself to be primarily a poet, although he had already experimented in several other literary genres. As well as the critical essay on Joyce, he had published a study of Proust in 1931 and had collaborated in a translation of the 'Anna Livia Plurabelle' episode from Joyce's *Finnegans Wake*.††

There were dramatic beginnings also, while at Trinity College. Two brief dialogues appeared in the college newspaper,‡ while his first play *Le Kid*‡‡ (a parody of *Le Cid*, by the classical French dramatist, Corneille (1606–84)) was written with a colleague, Georges Pelorson, for a Trinity College Modern Language Society production in 1931. Beckett also acted in this production.

Such works were written for amusement only and it was to fiction that Beckett turned on giving up his job at Trinity College. A short story, 'Assumption', had been published in 1929.§ Beckett now tried his hand at a full-length novel, *Dream of Fair to Middling Women*. The latter remains unpublished (apart from a few isolated passages) although a volume of short stories *More Pricks Than Kicks* (London, 1934) was largely abstracted from it. Belacqua, the hero of this early fiction, is named after the slothful figure in Dante's *Purgatorio*, with whom Beckett evidently identified himself at this time.§§ He had steeped him-

*Richard Ellmann, *James Joyce*, Oxford University Press, Oxford, 1959, p.661.

**Our Exagmination Round his Factification for Incamination of Work in Progress*, Paris, 1929; reprinted by Faber, London, 1972, pp.3–22.

†Richard N. Coe, *Beckett*, Oliver & Boyd, Edinburgh & London, 1964, p.12.

††*Nouvelle Revue Francaise*, Vol. 19 (1931), pp.633–46.

‡*T.C.D.: A College Miscellany*, 14 November 1929 and 12 March 1931.

‡‡Manuscript lost.

§*transition*, nos. 16 and 17 (Paris, 1929), pp.268–71.

§§Dante Alighieri (1265–1321). His *Divina Commedia* (*Inferno, Purgatorio, Paradiso*) was written between c.1308 and c.1320.

self in Dante while an undergraduate, and an apparently issueless purgatory is the locale of many of his later plays.

Beckett wrote his next novel, *Murphy* (London, 1938), during the period of rootlessness and uncertainty that followed his decision to abandon an academic career and also to make a life for himself outside Ireland. 'I didn't like living in Ireland,' said Beckett in an interview with Israel Shenker in 1956. 'You know the kind of thing—theocracy, censorship of books . . . I preferred to live abroad.'* Thus, in the autumn of 1937, he decided to settle permanently in Paris.

The outbreak of war in 1939 found Beckett visiting Dublin. He returned to Paris at once, preferring France at war to Ireland at peace. In 1940 he joined the Resistance, and in 1942, forewarned by a friend, left his flat in Paris only hours before the Nazis broke into it. He spent the next two years in the South of France living in seclusion, at times working as an agricultural labourer. In 1945 he was awarded the Croix de Guerre with a gold star for his 'great courage' and 'effectiveness as an information source in an important intelligence network'.**

While living his life of seclusion in 1942-4 Beckett began writing more experimental fiction than hitherto and the novel *Watt* (Paris, 1953) resulted. After the war, released apparently both by the freedom to write and by the decision to make French his first language, a period of astonishing creativity began for Beckett. His first discarded attempts at a novel in French culminated in the trilogy of novels, his most sustained and ambitious work in fiction.†

It was while writing the trilogy that he turned to the theatre 'as a relaxation' from the draining effect the novels were having on him.†† Thus his first real play, *Eleuthéria*, was written in 1947, the same year as *Molloy*, and *En attendant Godot* (*Waiting for Godot*) was written in 1948, the year of *Malone Meurt* (*Malone Dies*). The idea of writing plays as relaxation was clearly an extension of the light-hearted Trinity College parodies. Beckett did not at this stage see himself as a dramatist, but as a novelist, encumbered with the artist's 'obligation to express', though with no power to say anything and nothing to say. Such is the dilemma described in 'Tal Coat', the first of Beckett's three 'dialogues' with Georges Duthuit (editor of the magazine *transition*) which were published in 1949, the year he completed the trilogy, with *L'Innommable* (*The Unnamable*).‡

New York Times, 6 May 1956, Section 2 (X), p.1.
**Deirdre Bair, *Samuel Beckett*, Cape, London, 1978, p.319.
† *Molloy*, Éditions de Minuit, Paris, 1951; *Malone Meurt*, Éditions de Minuit, Paris, 1951; *L'Innommable*, Éditions de Minuit, Paris, 1953.
†† *En attendant Godot*, ed. Colin Duckworth, Harrap, London, 1966, p.xlv. All references in these Notes to the text of *En attendant Godot* refer to this edition.
‡ *transition Forty-Nine*, no.5 (Paris, 1949), pp.97-103.

The enormous effort of writing the three novels had exhausted Beckett's fictional voice, or rather, having deliberately destroyed conventional form in these novels, he appeared to have left himself nowhere further to go. He was still struggling with the problem seven years later, when interviewed by Israel Shenker:

> In the last book—L'Innommable—there's complete disintegration. No 'I', no 'have', no 'being'. No nominative, no accusative, no verb. There's no way to go on. The very last thing I wrote—Textes pour rien—was an attempt to get out of the attitude of disintegration, but it failed.*

The interview with Shenker took place in May 1956, just before the completion of Fin de partie (Endgame). Beckett had already found his new direction, but still regarded himself as a novelist in a cul-de-sac. He had not yet fully realised the potentialities that the theatre offered him. Nor had he anticipated the new roads that would open out for him from the main dramatic highway, occupying his major attention for the next twenty years.

Beckett and the theatre

Beckett visited the theatre a good deal as a young man in Dublin, when the Irish Dramatic Movement was full of vigour. This was a movement led by the poet W.B. Yeats (1865-1939) and his friend Lady Gregory (1852-1932) to encourage plays written especially for Irish audiences, instead of Irish writers transporting their talents to London, as had been the case since the seventeenth century. Beckett had been impressed by the later plays of W.B. Yeats and plays by John Synge (1871-1909) and Sean O'Casey (1884-1964) at the Abbey Theatre, Dublin. 'I wouldn't suggest that G.B.S. is not a great play-wright, whatever that is when it's at home,' he replied, when asked to contribute an appreciation of George Bernard Shaw to the Shaw Centenary celebrations in Dublin:

> What I would do is give the whole unupsettable apple-
> cart for a sup of the Hawk's Well, or the Saints', or
> a whiff of Juno, to go no further.
> Sorry.**

It was not only in Ireland that Beckett had had first-hand experience of attempts to find new directions in the theatre. The revolutionary Théâtre Alfred Jarry had been founded in Paris by Antonin Artaud

* New York Times, 6 May 1956, Section 2 (X), pp.1,3.
** Samuel Beckett: an exhibition, ed. James Knowlson, Turret, London, 1971, p.14. (The plays referred to are Yeats's At The Hawk's Well, Synge's The Well of The Saints and O'Casey's Juno and the Paycock.)

(1896–1948) and Roger Vitrac (1889–1952) in 1926, shortly before Beckett's arrival at the École Normale Supérieure. Artaud advocated a theatre in which the audience 'would no longer come merely to see but to participate', and challenged conventional theatrical subservience to the script. 'Theatre must be thrown back into life,' he demanded, envisaging an audience that would come to the theatre prepared as for an ordeal (like visiting the dentist) and would feel that 'we are capable of making them cry out'.* Beckett makes very similar demands on his audiences, requiring their active participation, in order to respond to his unconventional plots and dramatic images. A Beckett audience is thus (like an Artaud audience) subjected to a gruelling dramatic experience.

Roger Blin, the director to whom Beckett sent his first two plays, had worked closely with Artaud, in his Théâtre de la Cruauté (a further attempt to embody his dramatic ideas)** in the mid-thirties. Beckett chose Blin after admiring his 1949 production of *The Ghost Sonata*, a play by August Strindberg (1849–1912). Beckett sent *Eleuthéria* and *En attendant Godot* to Blin towards the end of 1949. Blin accepted both plays, but *Waiting for Godot* was finally selected for production because its five characters and minimal set were a much cheaper proposition than the seventeen characters and divided set of *Eleuthéria*. Even so, financial problems prevented *Waiting for Godot* from reaching the Paris stage until January 1953.

By the time Beckett wrote *Eleuthéria* and *Waiting for Godot*, he was already middle-aged and a mature novelist. Since he turned to the theatre for relief from the strain of writing novels, we would expect to find evidence of this in the still unpublished *Eleuthéria* (a Greek word, meaning 'freedom'). The play does not lack verbal humour, but, perhaps surprisingly, since Beckett was a devotee of the action-packed silent cinema, there is little dramatic action in *Eleuthéria*.

It is a play of three acts, in which Beckett relies too heavily on words (the tools of the novelist) and gives too little scope to what may be presented directly to the eye, by means of the stage picture. The latter, moreover, suffers from an unconventional division of the set. The stage is split into two separate scenes: the family household, and the bed-sitting-room of the son of the house, Victor Krap. There is no dividing wall. The two sets exist separately and yet are connected, emphasising the family web from which Victor (in leaving home, in his quest for freedom) has not escaped.

John Fletcher and John Spurling make the observation that in Beckett's subsequent plays, the divisions between the various pairs of

*Ronald Hayman, *Artaud And After*, Oxford University Press, Oxford, 1977, p.67.
**See Martin Esslin, *The Theatre of the Absurd*, revised edition, Pelican Books, Harmondsworth, 1977, pp.372–5.

characters 'are built into the whole theatrical effect and express the barrier between two sealed-off views of the world far more clearly than a mere splitting of the stage area'.* This is already evident in the pairs of characters in *Waiting for Godot*, written only a year after *Eleuthéria*. The play is an extraordinary example of dramatic craftsmanship, fusing language with action, the aural with the visual, in a beautifully controlled and balanced structure. By *Fin de Partie*, his next play, Beckett had become more daring. The play begins as a pattern of opposites, in the manner of *Waiting for Godot*; Hamm, for example, cannot stand up, while Clov cannot sit down. But gradually the relief of contrast is swallowed up, as the intensity of the play is increased.

For more than two decades Beckett has been writing his plays in English as a first language. Some minor short plays of the sixties were written first in French, but his main dramatic output has been written consistently in English since he was approached by BBC radio in June 1956, asking whether he would write a piece for the Third Programme. The radio play *All that Fall* was written within three months of this suggestion and the radio experience not only encouraged Beckett to write further works for broadcasting, but also influenced his next stage play, *Krapp's Last Tape* (1958). Further involvement with different dramatic media came with his film *Film* in 1963, followed, two years later, by the television play *Eh Joe*. Beckett's most recent plays (*Ghost Trio* and . . . *but the clouds* . . .) were also written for television.

The stage plays after *Happy Days* (1961) form a group in which, as the text becomes more brief, the dramatic images become bolder; and the precision with which Beckett shapes his work is strikingly evident. In *Waiting for Godot* and *Happy Days*, repetition of language and action is carefully balanced between the two acts of each play. By the time Beckett wrote the 121-word *Come and Go* (1965), however, he had dispensed with all text but the bones of the play, so that it is *all* shape, and has the effect of an enacted ritual.

The theatre has, then, in its various forms, dominated Beckett's writing since the completion of *L'Innommable* in 1949. One more novel, *Comment c'est* (translated as *How It Is*, London, 1964) appeared in Paris in 1961, since when his prose has become ever more spare, paralleling the shrinking size of his works for the stage. Beckett has kept to French as the first language for this dwindling fictional output.

The influence of radio, which caused Beckett to return to writing in English, seems to have encouraged him also to return to the stream of consciousness form of his novels. Since *All that Fall* his plays, with few exceptions, have been monologues of various kinds, voices in the head.

---

*John Fletcher and John Spurling, *Beckett, a study of his plays*, Eyre Methuen, London, 1972, p.49.

A note on the text

Waiting for Godot was written in French. In a detailed study of the play (which is essential reading for students) Colin Duckworth discusses the original manuscript, a closely written notebook, still in Beckett's possession.*

The play seems to have been written fluently ('I didn't have too much trouble with it,' remarked Beckett),** whereas most of his subsequent plays developed gradually, through numerous drafts. It is likely that *Waiting for Godot* was written the more easily, because the way had been prepared in earlier works. Beckett himself suggested that Duckworth should look at his first published novel: 'If you want to find the origins of *En attendant Godot*, look at *Murphy*.'† Duckworth also looked at the novel *Mercier et Camier* (written in 1945), tracing 'many coincidences of style and theme' between it and *Waiting for Godot*, and finding echoes from *Eleuthéria* as well.††

Thus, although there are no drafts of *Waiting for Godot* to consult, we can, to some extent, trace the evolution of the play from earlier works. Perhaps Duckworth's most interesting discoveries in the manuscript concern the withholding of information from the published text. Noticing, for example, a particular debt to Dante's *Purgatorio*, he remarks: 'Certain 'clues', then, have been progressively suppressed—clues which the reader of Dante will follow without hesitation (hence, no doubt, their suppression).'‡ In the manuscript version, moreover, Mr Godot definitely exists, in proof of which he sends a letter to Vladimir and Estragon. Beckett drew Duckworth's attention to a note in the manuscript about the identity of Godot, remarking that he had subsequently 'completely forgotten about it'.‡‡ This note states: 'Suggérer que Pozzo est peut-être Godot après tout, venu au rendez-vous, et qu'il ne sait pas que Vladimir et Estragon sont Vladimir et Estragon. Mais le messager?'§

The suppression of the written message from Mr Godot gives the play an extra dimension, as Beckett clearly realised, balancing it on the resultant ambiguity. *Ambiguity indeed becomes a keynote in Beckett's subsequent drama, and his work as a whole is fundamentally characterised by paradox.*

En attendant Godot, p.xlviii (note 1).
**Colin Duckworth, *Angels of Darkness*, Allen & Unwin, London, 1972, p.17.
† *En attendant Godot*, p.xlvi.
†† *En attendant Godot*, pp.xlviii, xlv–vi.
‡ *En attendant Godot*, p.lvii.
‡‡ *En attendant Godot*, pp.l–li, lx.
§ *En attendant Godot*, pp.lx–lxi. ('Suggest that Pozzo is perhaps Godot after all, come to the rendezvous, and that he doesn't know that Vladimir and Estragon are Vladimir and Estragon. But the messenger?')

En attendant Godot was first published in Paris in 1952. For the reprint of the play in 1953 a further piece of dialogue was added:

VLADIMIR: Qu'est-ce qu'il fait, Monsieur Godot? (*un temps*) Tu entends?
GARÇON: Oui Monsieur.
VLADIMIR: Et alors?
GARÇON: Il ne fait rien, Monsieur.
*Silence.**

In 1953–4 Beckett translated the play into English. It was first published in New York in 1954 and in London in 1956. The British censor objected, however, to certain passages and the complete text did not appear in England until 1965.

A number of differences distinguish the English version of the play from the original French text. Stage directions concerning the set are much clearer in the English text. Estragon sits on 'a low mound' (p.9), while he previously sat 'par terre' (p.3).** The tree 'has four or five leaves' (p.57) at the beginning of Act II, while the French text more vaguely states it to be 'couvert de feuilles' (p.49). The English text also introduces several new stage directions concerning the play's characters, specifying that Estragon speaks 'despairingly' (p.14) and 'violently' (p.20); and describing Pozzo as 'Sobbing' (p.46).

In much the same way as these directions specify the emotional state of Estragon and Pozzo, certain verbal changes help to clarify and emphasise the general context of the play. Estragon evokes his condition in terms of the word 'void' (p.66), while Vladimir refers to 'nothingness' (p.81). Both these terms are far more explicit than the original French expressions: respectively, 'le vide' (p.58), and 'des solitudes' (p.72).

It is significant that while Beckett's English text clarifies details concerning the set and general aspects of the characters' emotions and condition, it also lacks certain explanations present in the French version. Beckett cuts out a number of speeches, including details of Godot's home (p.14); the name of the fair to which Pozzo is taking Lucky (p.25); Pozzo's explanation of the term 'knouk' (p.27); the name of a farmer for whom Vladimir and Estragon worked (p.53); and details of people that Estragon has seen pass by (p.80).* The exclusion of these details makes the English text vaguer and more universal.

Beckett's use of English makes it impossible for him to employ certain aspects of word-play in the French text, such as the final confusion of 'relève' and 'enlève' (p.88). But the English text is enriched by word-play with such terms as 'waagerrim' (p.32), 'tray bong' (p.38),

* *Samuel Beckett: an exhibition*, ed. James Knowlson, p.62.

'The Hard Stool' (p.40), 'deadbeat' (p.46) and 'Crritic!' (p.75). (See the detailed summaries in Part 2 for a discussion of this word-play.)

Vladimir's and Estragon's expressions also become far more 'literary' in the English text. The colloquial 'Je commence à le croire' (p.3) becomes the more elegant statement, 'I'm beginning to come round to that opinion' (p.9); just as 'Tôt ou tard' (p.73) becomes 'In the fullness of time' (p.82). Vladimir quotes from the Bible (p.10), and Estragon echoes the poet Shelley (p.52). As the detailed summaries in Part 2 indicate, the English text also allows Beckett to use a number of Irishisms.

Part 2

Summaries
of WAITING FOR GODOT

A general summary

Act I

The scene is a country road, the scenery a tree and a low mound.
Estragon is sitting on the mound, trying to take off his boot. Vladimir
enters and they talk. Vladimir removes his hat several times during
their dialogue, peering inside it, as if he suspected something was there.
Estragon, having finally removed his boot, searches inside it in a similar
fashion. When Estragon suggests leaving, Vladimir replies, 'We can't
. . . We're waiting for Godot.' It soon becomes evident that the two
men have no precise information about Godot's arrival. They discuss
how to pass the time while waiting and consider hanging themselves
from the tree. The idea is abandoned after they reflect that only one of
them might succeed in dying, leaving the other alone.

Vladimir gives Estragon a turnip, followed by a carrot. While he is
eating the latter, Pozzo and Lucky enter. Lucky, carrying a lot of
luggage, is haltered by a long rope. The rope is held by Pozzo, who also
carries a whip. Lucky crosses the stage and goes out, but Pozzo, having
seen Vladimir and Estragon, stops suddenly, causing Lucky to fall over.
Vladimir and Estragon inquire whether Pozzo is Godot. Pozzo informs
them that they are waiting for Godot on his (Pozzo's) land. He then sits
down to a picnic, while Lucky remains holding the luggage.

When Pozzo has finished eating, Vladimir comments that his treatment of Lucky is scandalous, while Estragon asks why he does not put
down his burdens. Pozzo says that Lucky is probably trying to impress
him, so that he will not sell him at the fair. Creatures such as Lucky
should be killed, he says. Lucky weeps, but, when Estragon goes to
wipe his eyes, he kicks him violently, so that his leg bleeds. Vladimir
continues to reproach Pozzo for thinking of discarding such a 'faithful
servant'; but when Pozzo says that he can no longer tolerate Lucky's
terrible behaviour, Vladimir at once reproaches Lucky for ill-treating
his 'good master'!

Pozzo, having asked Estragon to persuade him to sit down, makes a
speech about the sky, for which he demands praise. When Vladimir
and Estragon congratulate him, he decides that Lucky should provide

them with some entertainment. Lucky dances briefly, twice, and is imitated by Estragon. Then, after Vladimir has provided him with his hat, he 'thinks' aloud, in a long tirade. This continues until Vladimir removes the offending hat and Lucky falls over. Vladimir and Estragon hoist him to his feet, but since he falls again as soon as he is unsupported, they are forced to hold him between them.

Pozzo brings over Lucky's burdens, which at first he drops. As soon as Lucky has grasped them, Vladimir and Estragon release Lucky and Pozzo tries out his paces with the whip. As he is about to leave, Pozzo discovers he has lost his watch. Pozzo and Lucky then depart, Lucky falling over again when Pozzo stops suddenly to collect the stool.

While Vladimir is wondering whether he has met Pozzo and Lucky before, since Estragon does not remember them, a Boy enters with the message that Mr Godot 'won't come this evening but surely tomorrow'. He says he is Mr Godot's goatherd and that his master is kind to him, but beats his brother, the shepherd. Vladimir asks the Boy to tell Mr Godot that he has seen them.

As soon as the Boy has gone, the light fails and the moon rises. Estragon removes his boots and places them at the edge of the stage. Vladimir tries to lead him away, but Estragon first contemplates the potential of the tree for committing suicide. He then goes to sit on the mound, reflecting whether they might be better off if they separated. Vladimir joins him, offering to part if Estragon wishes it. Estragon decides it is 'not worth while now' and suggests leaving. Vladimir agrees, but neither of them moves.

Act II

It is the next day, the same time and place as before. The tree has sprouted four or five leaves. Vladimir enters and walks about agitatedly, pausing to sing a song. Estragon enters barefoot. He has been beaten. The two men embrace. They pass the time in speech 'since we are incapable of keeping silent', and discuss whether to develop the dialogue by contradicting or questioning each other. When silence overtakes them, they take off their hats in order to think of a further topic.

Vladimir discusses the previous day, of which Estragon remembers nothing until prompted. In order to prove the truth of his remarks, Vladimir pulls up Estragon's trousers and shows him the wound from Lucky's kick. He also points out Estragon's boots, but Estragon denies that they are his. Eventually he allows Vladimir to help him try them on. Estragon then sits on the mound, while Vladimir sings him a lullaby. He goes to sleep and Vladimir covers him with his own coat. He soon awakens after a nightmare, however. Vladimir will not listen to the nightmare, but helps Estragon to 'walk it off'.

When Estragon starts complaining, Vladimir speaks roughly to him and Estragon decides to leave. Vladimir finds Lucky's hat and puts it on in place of his own, which he gives to Estragon. A comic routine of exchanging hats ensues, ending with Vladimir in Lucky's hat, Estragon in his own hat and Vladimir's hat discarded. Vladimir tries to entertain Estragon by imitating Lucky, asking him to play Pozzo. When Vladimir begins to dance, Estragon goes out, but returns at once, saying, 'They're coming!' He exits at the other side of the stage, but returns because 'They're coming there too!'

Vladimir suggests that Estragon should leave through the auditorium. Estragon recoils from this and attempts, unsuccessfully, to hide behind the tree. Both men then take up watching positions at the extreme left and right of the stage. Observing nothing, they begin to abuse each other. After Vladimir has been vanquished by the word 'Crritic!', the two men embrace. They decide to occupy themselves in physical exercise, first hopping and then standing on one leg, imitating the tree. Estragon staggers, brandishes his fists and yells, 'God have pity on me!'

Pozzo and Lucky enter, Lucky laden as before, but on a shorter rein, since Pozzo is blind. He stops short on seeing Vladimir and Estragon, so that Pozzo bumps into him. They both fall over and lie helpless. Estragon mistakes Pozzo for Godot. Vladimir and Estragon pursue their own thoughts, ignoring Pozzo's cries for help, until he offers money. Vladimir decides at last that to help would be a welcome diversion from routine. In attempting to raise Pozzo, however, Vladimir himself falls over. Finding he cannot get up, he calls for help, but Estragon makes no effort to assist him, until he appears contented to remain on the ground. Then, in trying to raise Vladimir, Estragon falls over in his turn. Pozzo, struck by Vladimir, crawls away. Estragon calls to him and, finding that he answers to the names of Abel and Cain, concludes, 'He's all humanity.'

Vladimir and Estragon get up without difficulty after this. They decide at last to assist Pozzo, who falls over as soon as they release him, so that they are forced to support him between them. Stuck with him thus, they question him about his blindness. Pozzo in turn wishes to know where he is and the time of day. He asks Estragon to discover whether Lucky is hurt, suggesting that he should first try him with the rope, and kick him if he gets no response. Estragon ascertains that Lucky is breathing and then kicks him until his foot hurts. He goes to the mound to try to remove his boot, but soon falls asleep.

Vladimir tries to discuss their previous encounter, but Pozzo has forgotten it and calls to Lucky to prepare for their departure. Vladimir asks for a song from Lucky before they leave, but Pozzo replies that he is dumb. Questioned by an incredulous Vladimir, Pozzo loses his temper and, in a diatribe against time, contrasts the brief gleam of human life with the long night of eternity. Pozzo and Lucky leave the stage, and are at once heard to fall again.

Vladimir awakens Estragon, who finds his boots still hurting him. After attempting to remove them, he dozes off again. Vladimir tries to assess the nature of reality, reflecting that most people pass through life as though asleep, never really getting to grips with the truth of things. The Boy enters and states that it is his first visit. Vladimir anticipates his message: Mr Godot will come tomorrow, 'without fail'. Mr Godot has no occupation; the Boy states when asked, 'He does nothing, sir.' Vladimir can think of no better message to send him than that of the previous evening: 'Tell him you saw me.' Afraid that the Boy will not recognise him the following day, he springs towards him, but the Boy evades him and runs out.

The sun sets immediately, as before, and the moon rises. Vladimir stands bowed and motionless. Estragon awakens, removes his boots, and places them centre front of the stage. Both men decide to leave, but Vladimir points out that they are obliged to return on the morrow, 'to wait for Godot'. They look at the tree, but again have no rope. Estragon remembers the cord supporting his trousers. He unties it and his trousers fall down. The two men test the strength of the cord, which breaks, so that they almost fall. They resolve to bring 'a good bit of rope' the following day. Estragon again considers parting from Vladimir, but Vladimir points out that if Godot does not come to save them, they can indeed hang themselves. He tells Estragon to pull on his trousers and suggests they leave. Estragon agrees, but, as at the end of Act I, neither moves.

Detailed summaries

Since *Waiting for Godot* has no scene divisions, the text has been divided, for convenience, into sections of action and dialogue. While other methods of textual division are possible and there may be differing opinions as to where a particular sequence ends, the present arrangement reveals Beckett's careful attention to balance and contrast in constructing his text.

In Beckett's production of the play at the Schiller Theater, Berlin, in 1975 (a production seen at the Royal Court Theatre, London, in April 1976), it was precisely the balance achieved between contrasting and repeated elements in the play that made it especially memorable. Beckett's production notebooks make it clear that he was aiming, in production, to bring out the variety as well as the repetition inherent in the patterning of the text.

Passages for commentary are inserted between each portion of text, in order to define and elucidate each sequence the more clearly. Page references are to the revised and unexpurgated English edition (Faber, London, 1965). The latest reprint edition (Faber, London, 1978) is quoted. Unusual words and phrases are glossed, unless adequately defined in the *Concise Oxford Dictionary*.

ACT I

Pages 9–11 (*Estragon, sitting on a low mound* ... Vladimir: 'This is getting alarming.')

The scene is a country road, the scenery a tree and a low mound. Estragon is sitting on the mound, trying in vain to take off his boot. Vladimir enters and they talk. Some comic business follows, in which Vladimir takes off his hat three times and peers suspiciously inside it, before putting it on again. During these antics Estragon at last removes his boot, also peering inside it, but is unable to discover why it had pained him.

NOTES AND GLOSSARY:

Nothing to be done: the phrase becomes a refrain in the play. It is repeated by Vladimir, for example, just before the end of the first section of text

Get up till I embrace you: 'till' used in this manner is an Irishism

His Highness: Vladimir addresses Estragon ironically, as if he were of royal blood

And they didn't beat you?: it is never established who 'they' are, but Estragon is attacked each time he separates from Vladimir

Hand in hand from the top of the Eiffel Tower: Vladimir regrets their not having jumped from the top of the Eiffel Tower in Paris 'in the nineties', when they were more presentable. Now they are too scruffy to be admitted to the tower

if you had what I have: Vladimir has prostate trouble, the reason for his awkward gait (legs wide apart) and frequent exits to pass water

Hope deferred maketh the something sick: 'something' here means 'heart'; an attempt at a biblical quotation, Proverbs 13:12

Beckett immediately establishes a contrast between Vladimir's dissatisfaction with his hat and Estragon's with his boots. It can be seen as drawing attention to Vladimir's preoccupation with things of the mind and Estragon's with things of the body. Beckett pointed to this contrast in rehearsals for the 1975 Schiller Theater production. The diary of his assistant (Walter Asmus) quotes him as saying: 'Estragon is on the ground, he belongs to the stone.' (A stone was used instead of the mound in this production.) Beckett added: 'Vladimir is light, he is orientated towards the sky. He belongs to the tree.'*

Pages 11–13 (*Silence* ... Estragon: 'People are bloody ignorant apes.')

Vladimir initiates a discussion about the Bible, showing particular interest in the two thieves who were crucified with Christ. Estragon does not share his interest.

NOTES AND GLOSSARY:

One of the thieves was saved: Beckett has a passage from St Augustine in mind here, as he once quoted to Sir Harold Hobson, the theatre critic: 'Do not despair; one of the thieves was saved. Do not presume; one of the thieves was damned.' Beckett commented, 'That sentence has a wonderful shape.' He went on to point out that the equal chance of being 'saved' or 'damned' extended to Estragon's feet, hence his trouble with one boot**

Gogo: Vladimir and Estragon address each other by the diminutives 'Gogo' and 'Didi'

Our being born?: 'Man's greatest sin is to have been born' (a quotation from Pedro Calderón (1600–81), the Spanish dramatist; it is quoted by Beckett in *Proust*, 1970, p.67.†)

only one speaks of a thief being saved: only one of the four Gospels in the Bible (Luke 23:43) mentions the reward for one thief

Pages 13–15 (*He rises painfully* ... Vladimir: (*feebly*). 'All right.')

Estragon limps to the extreme left, right and centre of the stage, and gazes into the distance, contemplating their solitary situation. After regarding the auditorium with the cynical comment 'Inspiring prospects', he suggests leaving. But Vladimir replies, 'We can't . . . We're waiting for Godot.' It soon becomes apparent that they are uncertain of all details related to Godot's arrival and of where precisely they are to await him.

Theatre Quarterly, Vol. V, no.19 (London, 1975) p.21.
**International Theatre Annual*, no.1 (London, 1956), p.153.
†All page references to Beckett's *Proust* refer to the reprinted edition, Calder & Boyars, London, 1970, rather than to the rare first edition, London, 1931.

NOTES AND GLOSSARY:
He said by the tree: since Beckett has already introduced the story of the crucifixion, some critics associate 'the tree' with the cross

---

Pages 15–17 (*Estragon sits* ... **Vladimir: 'It's for the kidneys.'**)

Estragon sits on the mound and goes to sleep. Vladimir paces up and down, sometimes halting to gaze into the distance offstage. Feeling lonely, he awakens Estragon, but refuses to hear the details of his nightmare. Estragon tries to tell him a joke, but Vladimir hurries out to pass water. Estragon follows him to the edge of the stage, making encouraging gestures. Vladimir enters with bowed head, but Estragon coaxes him into an embrace.

NOTES AND GLOSSARY:
This one is enough for you?: Vladimir has refused to listen to Estragon's nightmare. Estragon supposes the universe is nightmare enough, without adding to it
cawm: parody of an English upper-class accent
You stink of garlic!: Estragon's feet also smell. Beckett typically undercuts a tender or lyrical passage by a descent to the mundane, vulgar or absurd

---

Pages 17–19 (*Silence. Estragon looks attentively at the tree* ... **Vladimir: (*distinctly*). 'We got rid of them.'**)

The two men discuss how to pass the time while waiting, and consider hanging themselves. They abandon the idea on realising that if the second suicide were to fail, one of them would be left alone. Their expectations of Godot are seen to be as vague as the time of his arrival.

NOTES AND GLOSSARY:
Where it falls mandrakes grow: a plant with a root thought to resemble the human form; popularly supposed to grow where human sperm has fallen
strike the iron before it freezes: Beckett enlivens the cliché 'strike while the iron is hot'
On our hands and knees: Vladimir deliberately misunderstands Estragon's inquiry, 'Where do we come in?' (What happens to us?) and answers him ironically that if they 'come in' (enter) at all, it will be crawling
Your Worship: Vladimir addresses Estragon as though he were an important citizen

Pages 19–21 (*Silence ...* Estragon: 'Like to finish it?')

Vladimir thinks he hears someone coming, but it is a false alarm. Far from being disappointed, the two men sigh with relief. Estragon remarks that he is hungry. Vladimir gives him a turnip, mistaking it for a carrot, and finally finds him a carrot. Estragon inquires whether they are tied to Godot. Vladimir replies that they are not, 'For the moment.'

NOTES AND GLOSSARY:

Tied to Godot?: despite Vladimir's rejection of this idea, the two men *are* tied to the act of waiting, and thus to Godot, the awaited. (Notice that a rope *literally ties* Lucky to Pozzo)

Pages 21–25 (*A terrible cry ... puts it down and begins to eat.*)

The offstage cry terrifies Vladimir and Estragon. It heralds the arrival of Pozzo and Lucky. Lucky, burdened with a heavy bag, folding stool, picnic basket and greatcoat, is haltered by a long rope. The rope is held by Pozzo, who also carries a whip. Lucky crosses the stage and goes out, but Pozzo, having noticed Vladimir and Estragon, stops suddenly. The noise of Lucky falling as the rope tautens is heard. Vladimir and Estragon inquire as to Pozzo's identity. Estragon thinks he is Godot. Pozzo remarks that they are awaiting Godot on his (Pozzo's) land. He then jerks the rope and Lucky enters backwards. Lucky laboriously helps Pozzo on with his coat, places the stool to his satisfaction and gives him the picnic basket. When Pozzo has removed some chicken and wine, he makes Lucky take back the basket and stand well away while he eats.

NOTES AND GLOSSARY:

the clap: venereal disease

The grotesque master and slave relationship that exists between Pozzo and Lucky is sometimes said to be representative of capitalism riding on the backs of the workers. No such explanation should be taken as the 'sole truth' of the play. The lifeblood of Beckett's work is its *ambiguity*.

The circus aspect of the relationship (with Pozzo as ringmaster, cracking his whip) carries on an idea already established by the comic action and dialogue 'routines' of Vladimir and Estragon.

Pages 25–27 (*Silence ... He puffs at his pipe.*)

Vladimir and Estragon circle about Lucky, who sags repeatedly, until the bag and basket he is still holding touch the ground. They discover a sore on his neck, where the rope has chafed him. When they begin to question Lucky, Pozzo tells them to leave him in peace, but immediately makes further demands on Lucky himself. Having finished eating, Pozzo lights his pipe. Estragon covets the chicken bones and, since Lucky makes no verbal objection, Pozzo lets Estragon take them.

NOTES AND GLOSSARY:
at his last gasp: near to death

Pages 27–32 (Vladimir: (*exploding*). 'It's a scandal!' ... *Lucky weeps*.)

Vladimir comments angrily that Pozzo's treatment of Lucky is 'a scandal'. Although Pozzo does not appear to mind the remark, he rises to leave, but at once wishes to smoke a further pipe and prolong the conversation. In order to overcome the difficulty of changing his mind, he gets Lucky to move the stool, then reseats himself and refills his pipe. Vladimir wishes to leave, but Pozzo engages him in conversation about the absent Godot. Estragon meanwhile inquires why Lucky does not put down his bags. Pozzo is delighted with the question, spraying his throat twice with a vaporiser in order to prepare himself to answer, and forgetting the question in the process. Pozzo suggests finally that Lucky is hoping to impress him by the worth of his service, so that he will not be sold at the fair. 'The best thing' to do with 'such creatures', he remarks, is to kill them. Lucky, listening, weeps.

NOTES AND GLOSSARY:
your immediate future: without being told so specifically, Pozzo has realised their dependence on Godot
Why doesn't he put down his bags?: Beckett frequently uses the technique of a question ignored, repeated, and the answer deferred until much later in the text
to cod me: to fool me (an Irishism)
Atlas, son of Jupiter!: Atlas, in Greek mythology, was son of Iapetus, not Jupiter. His punishment, after the revolt of the Titans, was to hold up the heavens unassisted
You waagerrim?: after being repeatedly ignored, Vladamir's question becomes distorted, and thus catches Pozzo's attention

---

Pages 32–34 (Estragon: 'He's crying' ... Pozzo: 'What have I done with my pipe?')

Estragon takes Pozzo's handkerchief, in order to wipe Lucky's eyes, but Lucky kicks him so violently in response that his leg bleeds. Pozzo points out that Estragon's pain has now replaced Lucky's. He goes on to remark that he learned all the 'beautiful things' he knows from 'my Lucky'. Their association began, he says, 'nearly sixty years ago', and he compliments himself on his youthful appearance compared with Lucky's. Pozzo asks Lucky to take off his hat, revealing his long white hair. He then removes his own hat, revealing a totally bald head. Vladimir continues to reproach Pozzo for being about to dismiss 'such an old and faithful servant'. But when Pozzo says he can no longer tolerate Lucky's terrible behaviour, Vladimir at once attacks Lucky—for cruelty to 'Such a good master!' Pozzo recovers himself and states that nothing he has said has been the truth.

NOTES AND GLOSSARY:

I told you he didn't like strangers: Pozzo urged Estragon to help Lucky despite knowing what the result would be

The tears of the world are a constant quantity: another example of the ambiguous balance between contrasts established in the play, a balance that saves one of Estragon's feet and damns the other

knook: a word invented by Beckett to refer to Lucky

All four wear bowlers: this elaborates the circus clown aspect of the characters, referred to earlier

What have I done with my pipe?: this is the first of Pozzo's possessions to disappear, mysteriously, from his pockets

---

Pages 34–38 (Vladimir: 'Charming evening ... *Long silence*.)

Vladimir goes out to pass water, watched this time by Pozzo as well as Estragon. When he returns he walks about agitatedly, kicking over the stool, but gradually becomes calmer. Pozzo persuades Estragon to invite him to sit down, but no sooner has he done so than he consults his watch and decides it is time to leave. He resolves to inform Vladimir and Estragon about the twilights in 'these parts' before leaving. Vladimir is fiddling with his hat, Estragon with his boot, Lucky is half asleep, so Pozzo cracks his whip for attention, finally standing up to achieve a more effective sound. Invited by Estragon, he sits down again to make his speech about the sky.

NOTES AND GLOSSARY:

briar: a pipe, the bowl made of briar wood

dudeen: the Irish word (in general use in Ireland) for a clay pipe

Kapp and Peterson: a pipe, called after its manufacturers

Pan: Greek god (half man, half goat); the spirit of nature

Time has stopped: Act II shows that this is so for Vladimir and Estragon, but not for Pozzo and Lucky

Adam: Estragon here takes the name of the first man, in the Bible story. In Act II he calls Pozzo by the names of Adam's two sons, Cain and Abel

Qua sky: (*Latin*) 'As sky'

Pages 38–41 (Estragon: 'So long as one knows ... Pozzo: 'True!')

Pozzo demands praise for his speech. When it is given, he offers to do anything he can for Vladimir and Estragon in return. Estragon asks for money, but is ignored. Pozzo decides that Lucky should entertain them. Given the choice of seeing Lucky 'dance, or sing, or recite, or think', Estragon asks if he might 'dance first and think afterwards'. Lucky dances briefly, twice. Estragon imitates him and almost falls over. Lucky tries, unsuccessfully, to return to his burdens. Pozzo loses his train of thought, so all three men take off their hats simultaneously (Lucky's hat is already off) in order to concentrate. Estragon is stimulated to inquire, 'Why doesn't he put down his bags?' Vladimir points out that not only has Pozzo already answered this question, but Lucky *has* put down his bags, in order to dance.

NOTES AND GLOSSARY:

tray bong: bilingual joke, parodying an Englishman's pronunciation of the French *très bon* (very good)

Even five: Pozzo is oblivious of Estragon's financial requests. The situation is reversed, ironically, in Act II, where Pozzo offers money in return for assistance, whereupon Estragon hears his cries for help, as though for the first time

the farandole ...: traditional dances

The Hard Stool: constipation. Beckett uses the same joke ('the iron stool') in *Krapp's Last Tape*

pulverizer: refers to the vaporiser last used on page 37

My left lung is very weak!: the state of Estragon's lungs offers yet another example of the ambiguous balance between positive and negative realities in the play. (Compare with the state of his feet)

Pages 41–45 (*Silence. They put on their hats ... Silence. Panting of the victors.*)

Vladimir recalls that Lucky has not yet thought for them. Pozzo says he must have his hat first, so Vladimir puts it on for him, but he neither moves nor speaks. Pozzo asks Vladimir and Estragon to stand back. He then jerks Lucky's rope and asks him to think. Lucky begins to dance. Pozzo stops him, asking him again to think. Lucky begins speaking, but Pozzo stops him at once, making him turn towards the auditorium before resuming. Lucky thinks aloud, in a long 'tirade'. During the tirade Vladimir and Estragon alternate between periods of interest and periods of protest. Pozzo is alienated throughout. All three finally try to silence Lucky, but this proves ineffectual until Vladimir, urged by Pozzo, removes Lucky's hat. Lucky falls down.

NOTES AND GLOSSARY:

He can't think without his hat: in ironic contrast to the other three, who have just removed their hats in order to concentrate. A tenuous connection between the hat and things of the mind is suggested at the opening of the play (see p.18 of these Notes)

Lucky's tirade: When rehearsing the play in Berlin in 1975, Beckett began with Lucky's speech, as though it contained the core of the play. The rehearsal diary kept by his assistant director, Walter Asmus, quotes Beckett's approach to the speech: 'We are going to divide it into three parts and the second part is going to be divided again into two sections. The first part is about the indifference of heaven, about divine apathy. This part ends with, 'but not so fast . . .' The second part starts off with 'considering what is more', and is about man, who is shrinking—man who is dwindling. Not only the dwindling is important here, but the shrinking, too. These two points represent the two under-sections of the second part. The theme of the third part is 'the earth abode of stones' and starts with 'considering what is more, much more grave.'*

quaquaquaqua: Duckworth remarks that the manuscript has 'quoique' (although). In Berlin Beckett remarked: 'It concerns a god who turns himself in all directions at the same time. Lucky wants to say "Quaquaquaquaversalis" but he can't bring it out. He says instead only "quaquaquaqua".'** J. Blakey describes the result as a 'quacking sound, adding a derisive note to the speech'†

*Theatre Quarterly, Vol. V, no.19, p.22.
**Theatre Quarterly, Vol. V, no.19, p.22.
† Waiting for Godot: Notes, Coles, Toronto, 1972, p.22.

apathia: apathy; insensibility to suffering
athambia: imperturbability
aphasia: loss of speech, resulting from brain disease
the divine Miranda: Miranda in Shakespeare's *The Tempest*
Acacacacademy of Anthropopopometry: 'caca' and 'popo' are childish French words 'for excrement and chamberpot respectively'*
Essy-in-Possy: (*Latin*) *esse* (to be); *posse* (to be able)
Testew ... Cunard ... Fartov ... Belcher: 'invented names of vulgar origin'**
man ... is seen to waste and pine: the central statement in Lucky's speech
camogie: Irish sport (a kind of hockey)
Feckham Peckham Fulham Clapham: Feckham is an invention; the remaining names are all areas of London
Bishop Berkeley: Irish philosopher (1685–1753) admired by Beckett, who used one of Berkeley's precepts '*esse est percipi*' (to be is to be perceived) as the starting-point for his silent film, *Film*
Connemara: coastal region of Galway, in the West of Ireland
Steinweg and Peterman: names based on stone: Steinweg (German, Stoneroad); Peterman (biblical, Rockman). The theme of the third section of Lucky's speech is 'the earth abode of stones'

The incoherence of Lucky's speech seems to exemplify Beckett's pessimistic attitude towards language. The same kind of verbal chaos can be found in his more recent play *Not I* (London, 1973). Like Winnie in *Happy Days*, Lucky finds that 'words fail'.

Pages 45–48 (Estragon: 'Avenged!' ... *Long silence.*)

Vladimir peers inside Lucky's hat, until Pozzo snatches it from him and tramples it underfoot. Vladimir and Estragon hoist Lucky to his feet, but he falls over as soon as they let him go. They raise him again and hold him up. Pozzo brings over the bag and basket. Lucky drops both at first, but finally manages to hold on to them. Vladimir and Estragon release him, and this time he succeeds in remaining on his feet. Pozzo tries out his paces with the whip. As he is about to leave, Pozzo discovers he has lost his watch. Vladimir and Estragon listen to his stomach, in an attempt to locate the watch, but it is not found. Pozzo is unable to leave until he takes a running start. As on their arrival, Lucky

---

*See Fletcher, Fletcher, Smith and Bachem, *A Student's Guide to the Plays of Samuel Beckett*, Faber, London, 1978, p.62.
**Fletcher *et al.*, *A Student's Guide to the Plays of Samuel Beckett*, p.62.

falls over as soon as he is out of sight because Pozzo, having noticed the stool left behind, stops to recover it. Vladimir passes him the stool and Pozzo tosses it towards Lucky. The two men are then heard to move off.

NOTES AND GLOSSARY:

There's an end to his thinking!: Lucky cannot think aloud once deprived of his hat

deadbeat escapement: the mechanical terms describing Pozzo's watch have also an ambiguous, allusive quality typical of Beckett's choice of words

---

Pages 48–52 (Vladimir: 'That passed the time' ... *exit running*.)

Vladimir reflects that the presence of Pozzo and Lucky has helped to pass the time, which now hangs heavily again. He speaks of the two men as though he had met them before, although Estragon has no recollection of so doing. While Vladimir is questioning the accuracy of his memory and Estragon is again complaining about his feet, a voice is heard offstage and a Boy enters timidly. He has a message from Mr Godot. Urged by Vladimir, the Boy confesses he has been waiting for some time, but was afraid of Pozzo and his whip. Estragon does not believe the Boy's statements and shakes him. He then goes to the mound and begins to remove his boots. Vladimir appears to recognise the Boy, but he says he has never been there before. His message is that Mr Godot will come tomorrow. He is Mr Godot's goatherd. His master is kind to him, he says, but beats his brother, the shepherd. Told to tell Mr Godot that he has seen Vladimir and Estragon, the Boy runs off.

NOTES AND GLOSSARY:

Only we can't: as we see in Act II, nothing has changed for Vladimir and Estragon, although much has altered for Pozzo and Lucky

Unless they're not the same: a possible reference to Proust's idea that the self constantly changes, even from day to day. Paraphrasing Proust's ideas, Beckett remarked, 'We are other, no longer what we were before the calamity of yesterday,' and 'The individual is a succession of individuals.'*

He minds the sheep: the fact that Mr Godot favours the goatherd but beats the shepherd, his brother, undercuts the view of the play sometimes taken, that Godot = God. God is described in the Bible as separating the sheep from the goats, or the good from the bad

*Beckett, *Proust*, pp.13, 19.

Pages 52–54 (*The light suddenly fails ... * Curtain).

The light fails, bringing immediate night and a moon. Estragon places his boots at the edge of the stage. When Vladimir points out that he cannot go barefoot, Estragon replies that Christ did. Vladimir says things are going to be better, for tomorrow Godot is 'sure to come'. He tries to lead Estragon away. Estragon contemplates the tree, deciding to bring some rope to hang himself the following day. He recalls an earlier suicide attempt, when he threw himself into the river Rhône, and Vladimir fished him out. Vladimir still wishes to leave, but Estragon goes to sit on the mound, debating whether they might do better to separate: 'We weren't made for the same road.' There is no clear answer to this. Vladimir goes to sit beside Estragon, offering to part, if he so wishes. But Estragon says it is now too late to do so, and suggests to Vladimir that they should leave. Vladimir agrees. Neither moves.

NOTES AND GLOSSARY:

Pale for weariness: opening lines of 'To the Moon', a poem by Percy Bysshe Shelley (1792–1822): 'Art thou pale for weariness/ Of climbing heaven and gazing on the earth . . .'

All my life I've compared myself to him: at the beginning of the play Estragon appeared to have little knowledge of the New Testament of the Bible

nothing is certain: one of the key statements in the play. Beckett's work relies on ambiguity

They do not move: the decision to leave, contradicted by the lack of action, is precisely repeated at the end of Act II, the only difference being that the speakers of the last two lines are reversed

ACT II

Pages 57–58 (*Estragon's boots front centre ... no longer supported, almost falls.*)

Act II is headed: 'Next Day. Same Time. Same Place' (p.55). The tree, bare in Act I, has sprouted 'four or five leaves'. Vladimir enters and walks about agitatedly, halting from time to time. Finally, in a loud voice, he begins to sing a repetitive song about the death of a dog. When it is over he resumes his pacing, until Estragon enters, barefoot, and with bowed head. When Estragon refuses to be embraced, Vladimir inquires whether he has been beaten. The two men finally embrace and Estragon almost falls over when Vladimir releases him.

NOTES AND GLOSSARY:

The tree has four or five leaves: the appearance of new leaves on the tree is a repetitive rather than a hopeful process. Beckett told Roger Blin that this change occurs, 'not to show hope or inspiration, but only to record the passage of time'.* In *Waiting for Godot* life recurs because it has to, but the sparse leafage holds little promise of improvement. Nothing has changed for Vladimir and Estragon, and the events of Act II largely parallel and repeat those of Act I. Vladimir's round-song, with which Act II opens, emphasises the cynical quality of the play

Pages 59–62 (Estragon: 'What a day!' ... *Silence. Vladimir sighs deeply.*)

The two men discuss how each has fared in the absence of the other. Solemnly they decide that they must be happy to be reunited. Vladimir points out the change in the tree. Estragon appears to have forgotten everything about the past, until prompted by Vladimir.

NOTES AND GLOSSARY:

What is there to recognize?: Estragon loses his temper because, to him, everything seems the same, and thus no particular place or event is memorable. We can appreciate his annoyance from observing the similarity between the two acts. Although small details such as the leaves bring minor changes, the basic situation of Estragon and Vladimir remains constant. As Vladimir remarks earlier, 'The essential doesn't change.' (p.21)

I've crawled about in the mud!: see Beckett's novel *Comment c'est*, translated as *How It Is*, in which the protagonist is *literally* crawling in the mud

this muckheap: Clov, in *Endgame*, also refers to the world as 'this muckheap'; while Krapp, in *Krapp's Last Tape*, refers to the world as 'this old muckball'

Tell me about the worms!: Estragon considers the present an absurdity, compared with the long future of death and decomposition

the Macon country: an area of France

the Cackon country!: a further pun using 'caca', the childish French word for excrement

*Quoted by Deirdre Bair in *Samuel Beckett*, p.383.

for a man called . . . : in the original French version, the man was called Bonnelly (the name of a farmer at Roussillon, in south-eastern France, from whom Beckett used to buy wine during the war)

down there everything is red!: the colour of the soil at Roussillon. This kind of reference typifies Beckett's occasional use of highly obscure autobiographical details in works which usually have the most vague and general context

---

Pages 62–65 (Vladimir: 'You're a hard man' . . . *Silence.*)

Vladimir points out the difficulty of getting on with Estragon, who states once more that it would be better for them to separate. As usual, however, they decide to pass the time in conversation. In a passage of great lyrical beauty, they discuss the universal human need for self-expression, even when life is over:

ESTRAGON: They talk about their lives.
VLADIMIR: To have lived is not enough for them.
ESTRAGON: They have to talk about it.
VLADIMIR: To be dead is not enough for them.
ESTRAGON: It is not sufficient.

Vladimir and Estragon seem to feel this same need, but they also find that they cannot express themselves adequately with language, as the next few lines reveal:

VLADIMIR: Say something!
ESTRAGON: I'm trying.
Long silence.
VLADIMIR: (*in anguish*). Say anything at all!

A little more time is passed in discussing what they should discuss, and whether to contradict or question each other. They then reflect on the terrors of thought.

NOTES AND GLOSSARY:
like the other: Estragon probably refers to Pozzo's remark about killing Lucky (showing that he has some memory after all); but implications of the crucifixion seem to be present when Vladimir responds, 'To every man his little cross.'
All the dead voices: Beckett's later plays (from *Play* (1963) onwards), are concerned with the recapitulations of dead voices

Yes, but you have to decide: Vladimir and Estragon experience difficulty not only in coming to a decision, but also in acting upon it when they have done so (as at the end of each act)

A charnel-house!: the mind is seen as a vault in which dead thoughts are stored

Que voulez-vous?: (*French*) what can you expect?

Pages 65–68 (Estragon: 'That wasn't such a bad little canter . . . Estragon: 'Not enough.' *Silence*.)

Conversation flags again. In the hope of finding a new topic, they remove their hats (as in Act I) in order to concentrate. No new topic presents itself, however, until Vladimir, recapitulating the evening's events, remembers the tree. He returns to his efforts to make Estragon recall the previous day's happenings. In order to prove his point, he makes Estragon submit to an inspection of his legs, and finds the wound, where Lucky had kicked him, 'Beginning to fester!' When he points out Estragon's boots, Estragon denies that they are his. Vladimir offers Estragon a radish, but, since it is black, he refuses to eat it.

NOTES AND GLOSSARY:

canter: Estragon refers to the conversation they have just managed to maintain

There's no lack of void: Estragon's response to the universe is always negative, especially when challenged by Vladimir's optimism (as here, when he describes the tree as 'covered with leaves'). The original French text read 'couvert de feuilles', but it was discovered at the first production in Paris in 1953 that fewer leaves were more effective dramatically. Vladimir's optimism before such minimal foliage is considerably more ironic

This is becoming really insignificant: compare with *Endgame*, where Hamm comments, 'This is deadly.'

Pages 68–70 (Vladimir: 'What about trying them?' . . . *to keep himself warm*.)

In order to pass the time Vladimir helps Estragon to try on the boots. Estragon says they are too big. He goes to sit on the mound, taking up a 'foetal posture' in the hope of going to sleep. Vladimir sings him a lullaby and he sleeps. Vladimir covers him with his own coat, walking up and down to keep himself warm.

NOTES AND GLOSSARY:

to give us the impression we exist: compare with Beckett's recent stage play, *Footfalls* (London, 1976), where May has to hear the sound of her feet, to try to register her existence

no laces!: Estragon's dislike of laces seems linked with his fear of being 'tied' to Godot

They're too big: Beckett's wry comment to Colin Duckworth was, 'The second day boots are no doubt same as first and Estragon's feet wasted, pined, shrunk and dwindled in interval. There's exegesis for you.'*

Vladimir gets up softly, takes off his coat and lays it across Estragon's shoulders: one of the relatively few explicit gestures of kindness in Beckett's plays. Compare with the Auditor's 'gesture of helpless compassion' in the more recent *Not I*

Pages 70–72 (*Estragon wakes with a start ... Estragon: 'I'm going.'* Silence.)

Estragon starts up from a nightmare and Vladimir takes him in his arms. As in Act I, Vladimir refuses to listen to the nightmare, but helps Estragon to 'walk it off'. Estragon soon tires. When he begins to complain, Vladimir speaks roughly to him and Estragon decides to leave. Vladimir, ignoring him, suddenly notices Lucky's hat, thus confirming his impression that they have come to the right place. He puts on the hat and hands his own hat to Estragon. Estragon puts on Vladimir's hat and hands his own to Vladimir. Vladimir puts on Estragon's hat. The comic clowning routine of exchanging hats continues for some time, ending with Vladimir in Lucky's hat, Estragon in his own hat and Vladimir's hat on the ground. Vladimir poses in Lucky's hat, then takes it off to peer inside it, as in Act I.

James Knowlson identifies this hat routine as the 'three hats for two heads' act, used, for example, by the comedians Laurel and Hardy, and by the Marx Brothers in the film *Duck Soup*.**

Pages 72–75 (Vladimir: 'Will you not play?' ... *They resume their watch.* Silence.)

Vladimir tries to distract Estragon by imitating Lucky. He asks Estragon to play Pozzo, but Estragon has forgotten him. When Vladimir begins to dance, Estragon goes out precipitately, but returns at once,

*En attendant Godot, p.99.
**Samuel Beckett: an exhibition, ed. James Knowlson, p.70.

saying, 'I'm accursed!' He enlarges on this statement with the information, 'They're coming!' Vladimir, delighted, thinks Godot is coming at last, but Estragon rushes out again at the opposite side of the stage. He returns immediately, as before, commenting, 'I'm in hell!' He goes on to observe that 'They're coming there too!' He has no idea who 'they' are. Vladimir, remarking that they are surrounded, drags Estragon from the back of the stage (whither he has been trying to escape) towards the auditorium. Estragon recoils from this in horror and attempts to hide behind the tree. When its protection proves entirely inadequate, Estragon gains control of himself and the two men take up positions to the extreme right and left of the stage. They scan the horizon, but see nothing.

NOTES AND GLOSSARY:

Gonococcus! Spirochaete!: the active elements in gonorrhoea and syphilis

There's no way out there: escape is impossible by going back, whether it be backstage or back in time (as in Estragon's recent adoption of the foetal posture (p.70), as if he hoped to return to the womb)

Gesture towards front: comedy is created at the expense of the audience, who seem to cause Estragon 'horror'. Beckett uses a similar comic technique in *Endgame*

Pages 75–77 (Vladimir: 'You must have had a vision' ... Estragon: 'On me! On me! Pity! On me!')

Still observing nothing, they begin to abuse each other. Estragon silences Vladimir with the insult 'Crritic!', whereupon they embrace. Caught again with nothing to do, they decide to occupy themselves with physical exercise. First they hop from foot to foot, then, in turn, imitate the tree by standing on one leg 'for the balance'. Estragon, staggering, stops his imitation to brandish his fists, yelling at the top of his voice, 'God have pity on me!'

NOTES AND GLOSSARY:

Morpion!: (*French*) pubic louse

Crritic!: the French text allows the actors to choose their own insults. (See *En attendant Godot*, p.99)

Do you think God sees me?: if the tree is considered to have implications of the cross, Estragon's question is particularly relevant, as also is the Bishop Berkeley dictum quoted earlier: 'To be is to be perceived.'

Pages 77–81 (*Enter Pozzo and Lucky ... stumbles, falls, tries to get up, fails.*)

Pozzo and Lucky enter. Lucky is laden as before, but on a much shorter rope, since Pozzo is blind. Lucky has another hat. He stops short on seeing Vladimir and Estragon, so that Pozzo bumps into him. As in Act I, Lucky falls, bringing Pozzo down with him: 'They lie helpless among the scattered baggage.' Estragon believes Godot has arrived, while Vladimir regards the newcomers as aids to pass the time. The two men pursue their own reflections, heedless of Pozzo's repeated cries for help. Estragon, finally convinced that Pozzo is not Godot but the donor of yesterday's bone, considers securing another before assisting him. Vladimir wonders whether Lucky will again resort to violence and resolves finally, 'Let us do something, while we have the chance! It is not every day that we are needed.' But instead of going straight to Pozzo's assistance, he continues to speculate: 'What are we doing here, *that* is the question. And we are blessed in this, that we happen to know the answer. Yes, in this immense confusion one thing alone is clear. We are waiting for Godot to come—.' Pozzo's cries are heard by Estragon as soon as he offers payment for assistance. At the same time Vladimir becomes aware that they are wasting a potential diversion and he attempts to help Pozzo. But he fails to pull him to his feet, falls over in his turn, and is unable to rise.

NOTES AND GLOSSARY:

ballocksed:　　vulgar slang, meaning 'done for' (roughly equivalent to the French text's use of 'baisés')

all mankind is us:　Vladimir voices the universal implications of the text, strongly felt throughout the play, but nowhere so explicitly put: 'At this place, at this moment of time, all mankind is us, whether we like it or not.'

pros and cons:　　(*Latin*) arguments for and against

congeners:　　kin

this immense confusion: Vladimir's description of existence emphasises the perceptual uncertainty from which both he and Estragon suffer

to prevent our reason from foundering: habit can become a means of shutting out the unpleasant facts of life. Beckett discusses habit in his study of Proust (pp.18–29), commenting that habit functions as 'the guarantee of a dull inviolability' (p.19). Vladimir likewise calls habit 'a great deadener' (p.91)

We are all born mad. Some remain so: Beckett is playing on the famous lines from Shakespeare's *Twelfth Night* (Act 3, scene 5): 'Some are born great, some achieve greatness, and some have greatness thrust upon 'em.'

Pages 81–82 (Estragon: 'What's the matter with you all?' ... *Long silence*.)

Vladimir calls for help. Estragon does not assist him. Instead he makes up his mind to leave, but does not. As soon as Vladimir seems contented to remain where he is, however, Estragon holds out his hand. But he fails to raise Vladimir and falls, in his turn, among the other bodies.

NOTES AND GLOSSARY:
Pyrenees: mountain range separating France from Spain

Pages 82–84 (Pozzo: 'Help!' ... Vladimir: 'Ah!' *Silence*.)

They all lie in a heap until Pozzo is struck by Vladimir, for an ambiguous offence. Pozzo crawls away and does not reply to Vladimir's call. Estragon decides to try him with other names, and, when Pozzo responds to both 'Abel' and 'Cain', concludes, 'He's all humanity.'

NOTES AND GLOSSARY:
saws the air blindly: gropes about in the air with his hand
I'm afraid he's dying: in Beckett's vocabulary living = dying, because birth is the first step towards death
Abel! ... Cain!: since the names of the sons of Adam are called from the heap of bodies on the floor, Beckett gives ironic emphasis to the plight of fallen mankind

---

Pages 84–88 (Estragon: 'Suppose we got up to begin with' ... *his head on his arms*.)

Having decided to get up, Vladimir and Estragon do so without difficulty. 'Simple question of will-power', says Vladimir. They decide at last to assist Pozzo, who falls as soon as they release him. They help him to his feet a second time and are forced to hold him up, as they did with Lucky in Act I. Blind Pozzo questions the identity of his rescuers and is anxious to know the time of day. Having assured him that it is evening, Vladimir and Estragon again try to let him go, but have to catch him as he falls. Since they cannot leave him, they question him about his blindness. 'I woke up one fine day as blind as Fortune,' Pozzo replies. Believing Pozzo to have been present and sighted the previous day, Vladimir tries to ascertain when the blindness occurred. Pozzo responds in anger that 'The blind have no notion of time.' He wishes to know where they are, wondering whether it is 'the place known as the Board'. 'It's indescribable. It's like nothing,' replies Vladimir. Pozzo inquires what has happened to Lucky and is told of their fall. Since he cannot be left alone, he asks one of them to see whether Lucky is hurt. It is decided that Estragon should go, since 'he stinks so.' Pozzo tells him first to pull on Lucky's rope, and, if this fails, to 'give him a taste of his boot, in the face and the privates as far as possible'. Having ascertained, on Vladimir's advice, that the recumbent Lucky is still living, Estragon kicks him violently, hurting his own foot in the process. He limps to the mound and attempts to remove his boot, but soon gives up and goes to sleep.

NOTES AND GLOSSARY:

highwaymen: commentators have alluded to the parable of the Good Samaritan (see Luke 10:30–7) at this reference, as also in relation to the nightly beating of Estragon. Pozzo, sagging between Vladimir and Estragon, 'his arms round their necks', may perhaps be seen as another image of crucified man, in a play that abounds in ironic references to the crucifixion of Christ

night is drawing nigh: from the hymn 'Now the day is over' by S. Baring-Gould, also quoted by Krapp in *Krapp's Last Tape*

Memoria praeteritorum bonorum: (*Latin*) 'Memory of past happiness'

the place known as the Board: possibly an ironic reference to the stage (sometimes described as 'the Boards'); 'the Board' seems to suggest an official body, and this may be a reference to the Board (the governing body) of Trinity College, Dublin. It is called 'a wart on the arse of creation' in a student song

No point in exerting yourself if he's dead: from this speech until the deliberate reversal of values in Estragon's 'Oh the brute!' the comedy becomes very black

---

Pages 88–89 (Pozzo: 'What's gone wrong now?' ... *they are down again. Silence.*)

Vladimir tries to discuss the previous day's encounter with Pozzo, but he, like Estragon, has forgotten it. He cuts short the discussion and calls to Lucky, who rises, gathering up his 'burdens'. But he is without foresight and has to put everything down again, twice, in order to hand Pozzo first the whip and then the rope. Vladimir requests a song from Lucky before they leave, but Pozzo objects that he is dumb. Vladimir is incredulous, asking, 'Since when?' This causes Pozzo to lose his temper in a furious diatribe against time, asking, 'One day, is that not enough for you, one day like any other day . . .' Pozzo concludes with a famous passage on the brevity of human life, seen against the wastes of time: 'They give birth astride of a grave, the light gleams an instant, then it's night once more.' As soon as Pozzo has finished speaking, he leaves, with Lucky; and, as in Act I, they are heard to fall as soon as they have left the stage.

NOTES AND GLOSSARY:

I don't remember having met anyone yesterday: only Vladimir has a working memory and he questions its accuracy at the end of Act I ('Unless they're not the same . . .' (p.48))

Pages 89–91 (*Vladimir goes towards Estragon . . . halts finally at extreme left, broods.*)

Vladimir shakes Estragon awake and, as before, refuses to hear his dream. Vladimir is absorbed by the fact that Pozzo appeared to have been able to see them, while Estragon returns to his suggestion that Pozzo is Godot. As Estragon dozes off again, after experiencing the usual difficulty with his boots, Vladimir restlessly considers the nature of reality: 'But in all that what truth will there be?' He reflects that he too may be 'sleeping now', speculates that he 'knows nothing', and then questions these very conclusions, asking, 'What have I said?'

NOTES AND GLOSSARY:

Are you sure it wasn't him?: Beckett once considered the possibility that Pozzo might turn out to be Godot, after all. (See p.11 of these Notes)

the grave-digger puts on the forceps: like Pozzo (who reflected, 'They give birth astride of a grave' (p.89)), Vladimir thinks of life in terms of closely related moments of birth and burial

habit is a great deadener: habitual actions form a kind of 'deadener' or pain-killer, protecting man from distressing aspects of reality

let him sleep on: compare Christ in Gethsemane (see Bible, Mark 14:41): 'Sleep on now, and take your rest.'

I can't go on: compare the last words of *The Unnamable* (the final volume of Beckett's trilogy of novels): 'You must go on, I can't go on, I'll go on.'

Pages 91–92 (*Enter Boy right ... exit running. Silence.*)

The Boy appears, as in Act I. He does not recognise Vladimir and says it is his first visit. With studied irony, Vladimir anticipates the Boy's message: Mr Godot cannot come today, but he will come tomorrow, 'without fail'. The Boy agrees that this indeed is what he was told to say. He has not seen Pozzo and Lucky. When Vladimir asks about Mr Godot's occupation, the Boy replies, 'He does nothing, sir.' He describes Godot as having a white beard, so far as he can judge. When asked for a message, Vladimir can only think of repeating that of the previous day: 'tell him you saw me and that ... (*he hesitates*) ... that you saw me.' Anticipating that the Boy will return the following day with no recollection of their present meeting, Vladimir suddenly springs towards him. But the Boy evades him and runs out.

NOTES AND GLOSSARY:

Off we go again: Vladimir emphasises the predictable circularity of the action

tell him you saw me: again the need to feel that one has been perceived, that one's existence has been acknowledged, is stressed

---

Pages 92–94 (*The sun sets, the moon rises ...* Curtain).

In the pause following the Boy's exit Vladimir stands motionless, with bowed head. Estragon wakes, removes his boots and places them centre front of the stage. Both men decide to leave, but Vladimir points out that they cannot go far, because of having to return the next day to resume their wait for Godot. They look at the tree and the idea of suicide presents itself once more, but, as before, they have no rope. Estragon remembers the cord supporting his trousers. He removes it and his trousers fall to the ground. The two men pull the cord to test its strength. It breaks—and they almost fall. As in Act I, Estragon resolves to bring 'a good bit of rope' the following day. Once more he considers parting, but Vladimir points out that if Godot does not come to 'save' them, they can hang themselves as planned. Vladimir takes off Lucky's hat, peers inside it, and replaces it on his head. He tells Estragon to pull up his fallen trousers. This done, Vladimir suggests leaving and Estragon agrees. But again, as in Act I, 'They do not move.'

NOTES AND GLOSSARY:

The sun sets, the moon rises: parody of naturalistic drama, as in Act I. This was particularly apparent in Beckett's 1975 Berlin production

puts them down centre front: in Act I the precise position of the boots was not specified. Beckett sets up a pattern of asymmetrical repetition, both of language and action, between Acts I and II, so that the impression is one of sameness with difference. The whole play is most carefully balanced between repetition and contrast, with always just enough variety introduced to lend new impetus to the action or dialogue

And if we dropped him?: compare Act I (p.20): 'We're not tied!'

A willow: the willow tree is traditionally called the 'weeping willow'

his trousers . . . fall about his ankles: this piece of circus clowning does not break audience concentration. The absurdity contributes to the sense of helplessness, of 'nothing to be done', that is so strongly felt as the play closes

I can't go on like this: Estragon echoes Vladimir's statement of p.91

We'll be saved: the text has come full circle. Compare Act I, where Vladimir reflects that 'One of the thieves was saved' (p.11). Vladimir also mentions that Godot is not entirely benevolent; if 'dropped' by Vladimir and Estragon 'He'd *punish* us' (p.93)

Vladimir takes off his hat: the action also has come full circle. In Act I, 'He takes off his hat, peers inside it, feels about inside it, shakes it, puts it on again' (p.10)

pull off my trousers? . . . Pull ON your trousers: a final example of the difficulties that Vladimir and Estragon encounter when attempting to communicate verbally. Estragon confuses the words 'off' and 'on' (a confusion that is even more striking in the original French text, where he mistakes the words 'relève' and 'enlève')

They do not move: Beckett completes his patterning by making both the language and the action of the final lines a precise repetition of the end of Act I, thus emphasising the endless circularity of the play. The one variation (the reversal of the speakers) shows clearly that no matter who takes the initiative, whether the thinking man or the physical man, the end result is the same. They may resolve to leave, but are incapable of so doing. They are indeed 'tied' to Godot

Part 3

Commentary

Beckett's literary background

If the general literary background of Beckett's youth can be said to be the literary era of 'Modernism' (approximately 1900 to 1930), then Beckett's own work may be seen to exemplify the subsequent era of 'Post-Modernism'. Post-Modernism is usually associated with the years from 1930 to the present day, and its major works nearly always modify the preoccupations of Modernism by reducing them to extreme forms, be these extremely simple *structures* or extremely simple *ideas*.

Modernism can best be introduced with reference to James Joyce and Marcel Proust, two of the literary 'giants' of this period, who are both known to have interested and influenced Beckett in the 1930s. Joyce's most famous work is *Ulysses* (1922), a novel with many unusual characteristics. Unlike the traditional novel, which often described the entire lives of its characters, *Ulysses* describes the meetings, conversations, thoughts and memories of its characters during one day in the city of Dublin. For Joyce, twenty-four hours contained more than enough material for a novel. In order to represent the complexity of all the different thoughts and events that fill this day, Joyce does not simply use a single narrational style (as the conventional novelist would have done), but employs an immense variety of verbal techniques, ranging from the ancient solemnity of biblical English to the incoherent observations of his characters' daydreams.

Briefly, *Ulysses* typifies a number of Modernist concerns, such as the complex quality of time; the intensity of certain momentary experiences; the immensity of the city; and the richness of language—a mode of communication that Joyce stretched to its very limits. Beckett himself has commented upon the enthusiastic way in which Joyce experimented with language, commenting that 'Joyce believed in words,' and remarking that, in Joyce's opinion, 'All you had to do was rearrange them and they would express what you wanted.'*

Although Modernist writers such as Joyce employed all kinds of language in optimistic attempts to describe the new realities of the early twentieth century, Post-Modern writers, such as Beckett, have con-

*Quoted by Lawrence E. Harvey in *Samuel Beckett, Poet and Critic*, Princeton University Press, Princeton, New Jersey, 1970, pp.249–50.

cluded that words only offer totally inadequate communication. Contrasting his approach to writing with that of Joyce, Beckett has commented: 'Joyce is a superb manipulator of material . . . He was making words do the absolute maximum of work . . . The kind of work I do is one in which I'm not master of my material . . . I'm working with impotence, ignorance.'* Beckett further argues that it is impossible to write successfully about contemporary reality because it usually seems quite inexplicable, and he concludes: 'anyone nowadays who pays the slightest attention to his own experience finds it the experience of a non-knower, a non-can-er (somebody who cannot).'** Typical of this thoroughly pessimistic attitude towards language and existence is Lucky's speech (pp.42–5), and Estragon's first statement: there is 'Nothing to be done' (p.9).

Like Joyce's *Ulysses*, Proust's *A la recherche du temps perdu* (*Remembrance of Things Past*) is a novel concerned with the complexity of society; the complexity of time; the complexity of language; and the complexity of perception. While Joyce's *Ulysses* describes innumerable aspects of working-class life and middle-class life in Dublin, Proust's novel gives special attention to the middle and upper classes of Paris, describing them in terms of the sensations of a young writer named Marcel. Like Joyce, Proust attempts to evoke the complexity of his characters' sensations by using language unconventionally. If Joyce mixes a number of different styles, Proust describes sensations with enormous sentences, some of which are more than a page in length. Typical of Proust's technique are the first six pages of his novel, which describe only the minute sensations of Marcel as he wakes up.

Proust seems to have written such detailed descriptions because he realised that people and objects often appear slightly different every time we see them. Indeed, instead of describing traditional characters who behave fairly consistently according to their 'type', Proust describes confusing characters who continually offer differing impressions to Marcel. In his early study *Proust*, Beckett reflects that for Proust, 'We are not merely more weary because of yesterday, we are other, no longer what we were . . . yesterday.'†

Like Proust, Beckett appears fascinated by the way in which things seem different every time they are seen. But just as Beckett shares Joyce's preoccupation with the limits of language, without sharing Joyce's confidence in the effectiveness of words, so too does Beckett share Proust's preoccupation with the limits of man's perceptions, without sharing Proust's belief that man may find solutions to the problems of perceiving reality adequately.

*Quoted by Israel Shenker, *New York Times*, 6 May 1956, Section 2 (X) p.3.
***New York Times*, 6 May 1956, Section 2 (X), p.3.
†Beckett, *Proust*, p.13.

Proust describes two solutions to the problem of perceptual confusion. The first and least valuable of these ways of finding perceptual
certainty is that of habit, that is, the 'certainty' we derive from things
that we do every day. For example, Marcel finds it easy to sleep at home,
because he sleeps in the familiar (rather than confusing) reality of his
'own little bed'. However, the certainty of this habitual reality is
challenged when Marcel goes on holiday and sleeps in a new, inhabitual
bed, in a strange room. For a long time Marcel finds this room un-
familiar and confusing, and is only able to sleep in it when it at last
becomes a familiar form of habitual reality.

In *Waiting for Godot*, Estragon and Vladimir bitterly regret that
'Nothing is certain' (p.53) as they wait in vain for Mr Godot to save
them. And like Proust's Marcel, Beckett's Vladimir remarks that
habitual actions offer some degree of certainty in an uncertain world,
commenting that 'Habit is a great deadener' (p.91). In other words,
habit 'deadens' the confusion that he might otherwise feel.

Beckett's study of Proust emphasises the way in which *time* causes
perceptual confusion by bringing about changes that challenge man's
habitual beliefs by making man 'other' than what he was 'yesterday'.
In much the same way, Vladimir and Estragon find that their habitual
certainties are challenged by every new day, and at the beginning of
Act II Vladimir comments, 'Things have changed here since yesterday'
(p.60).

The second form of certainty that Proust describes is one that seems
to transcend the problem of time, and the confusions between yesterday
and today. This form of certainty is the result of involuntary memory—
a form of sudden memories which unexpectedly remind Marcel of
sensations that he has previously experienced and then forgotten. These
sensations appear to evoke timeless realities that seem far more significant than the habitual realities he deliberately remembers, and at the
end of Proust's novel, Marcel decides to write a novel of his own to
commemorate the special joy that these unexpected memories provide.

Unlike Proust's Marcel, Beckett's Estragon and Vladimir do not
seem to enjoy any special memories. Indeed, rather than wishing to
record important experiences from the past, they seem most unwilling
to consider each other's memories. When Estragon tries to tell Vladimir
of his most vivid private experience—his nightmares—Vladimir refuses
to listen to him, and the following exchange occurs:

ESTRAGON: I had a dream.
VLADIMIR: Don't tell me!
ESTRAGON: I dreamt that—
VLADIMIR: DON'T TELL ME!
ESTRAGON: . . . It's not nice of you, Didi. Who am I to tell my private
nightmares to if I can't tell them to you?

VLADIMIR: Let them remain private. You know I can't bear that.
(pp.15–16)*

Although Estragon and Vladimir often seem aware that habitual certainties are far from perfect, they appear quite unwilling to contemplate the 'deeper' past realities that sudden memories and nightmares reveal. This would seem to be because the 'deep' reality of their world is always a source of pain and sorrow. Unlike Proust's Marcel, they never find that vivid memories are a source of special joy.

The difference between the rather negative deep reality of Beckett's world and the frequently positive deep reality of Proust's and Joyce's world is typical of the difference between Modernist and Post-Modernist writing. For while Modernist writers like Proust and Post-Modernist writers like Beckett share the same basic concern for such problems as the nature of language, the nature of time, the nature of perception and the nature of memory, their *conclusions* to these problems and their *representation* of these problems are often very different.

Waiting for Godot suggests that there is 'Nothing to be done', offering predominantly pessimistic conclusions to problems that Joyce and Proust examined far more optimistically. If this play's conclusions exemplify the way in which Post-Modern writers frequently *reduce* the optimism of Modernist writing to a fairly simplistic pessimism, the dramatic means with which Beckett represents his pessimistic vision also *simplify* many other characteristics of Modernist writing.

While Joyce and Proust chose to represent the immensity of such cities as Dublin or Paris, Beckett simplifies the location of *Waiting for Godot* to 'a low mound' (p.9) on 'a country road' (p.10). Rather than attempting to portray a specific social class, such as the lower-class characters in Joyce's *Ulysses* or the aristocrats described by Proust, Beckett's two main characters seem to be social outcasts, tramps who belong to no specific class, and whose simplicity seems to make them representative of all mankind. Instead of describing action that takes place over a prolonged period of time, as Proust does, Beckett simplifies the duration of *Waiting for Godot* to two days. In this respect, he at first seems to have much in common with a Modernist writer such as Joyce, whose *Ulysses* describes a twenty-four-hour period. But whereas Joyce fills these twenty-four hours with an enormous variety of complicated meetings and discussions between dozens of characters, Beckett simply presents two encounters between Estragon and Vladimir, and Pozzo, Lucky and a boy, as they wait in vain to meet Godot.

The overall simplicity of *Waiting for Godot* led the critic Vivian Mercier to describe it as 'a play in which nothing happens, *twice*'.** But

*Compare with p.70 and pp.89–90 of *Waiting for Godot*.
**Vivian Mercier, 'The Mathematical Limit', *The Nation*, CLXXXVIII (14 February 1959), pp.144–5.

despite the fact that Estragon likewise complains that 'Nothing happens, nobody comes, nobody goes, it's awful!' (p.41), our summary
clearly indicates that *Waiting for Godot* is a play in which *something*
happens twice. It seems extremely significant that this action, this
'something', should happen twice. Discussing *Waiting for Godot*, Beckett has commented that 'one act would have been too little and three
acts would have been too much'.* This comment can probably be
understood most easily in terms of Beckett's suggestion that 'the key
word in my plays is "perhaps"'.**

This second statement probably refers to Beckett's tendency to
reduce reality to simple, paradoxical situations which seem to lack any
final explanation. One example of this tendency is the problem of
Godot's arrival. Perhaps he will finally arrive, perhaps he will not.
Beckett offers no precise solution to this problem. In much the same
way, Pozzo finds no specific solution to the problem of pleasure and
pain. Instead of suggesting that the world may slowly be improved, and
transformed into a place where there will be more pleasure than pain,
Pozzo reflects that the fact that somebody has ceased to weep does not
necessarily mean that the world has changed, since: 'The tears of the
world are a constant quantity. For each one who begins to weep, some-
where else another stops' (p.33). In other words, there seem to be just
as many people beginning to weep as there are people who cease to
weep, and as a result it is impossible to say whether or not the world
has improved.

The two acts of *Waiting for Godot* offer the spectator a similar paradox. In each act some characters suffer, while other characters do not.
For example, the Boy in Act I claims that Mr Godot does not beat him,
but does beat his brother (p.51). Pozzo changes from being a powerful
bully in Act I to a helpless blind man in Act II. No explanation is given
for these paradoxical situations, and the general circumstances of the
characters are never remedied: Godot never arrives.

Two acts seem to offer the perfect structure for *Waiting for Godot*
because they allow Beckett to juxtapose ambiguous reversals of fortune
in a highly formal, balanced manner. Each act echoes the other, and as
a result Beckett manages to impose a certain formal pattern upon his
play, while also allowing it to have an entirely imprecise meaning. *The
form* of *Waiting for Godot* is very carefully *defined*, being, in Beckett's
terms, neither 'too little' nor 'too much'. But *the implications* of this
play are equally carefully *undefined*, offering a paradoxical situation
that can only be interpreted with the word 'perhaps'.

To conclude, *Waiting for Godot* can be said to occupy a position

*Quoted by Israel Shenker, *New York Times*, 6 May 1956, Section 2 (X) p.3.
**Quoted by Tom F. Driver, 'Beckett by the Madeleine', *Columbia University Forum*,
Vol. IV, Summer 1961, pp.21–5, 23.

between the different eras of Modernism and Post-Modernism. To some extent, this play can be considered to form an extension of Modernism, since it shares Joyce's preoccupation with language and Proust's preoccupation with time, perception and memories. But as a work which utterly rejects Joyce's confidence in language and Proust's confidence in involuntary memory, this pessimistic play is thoroughly Post-Modern in character. *Waiting for Godot* may also be said to be Post-Modern in terms of the way in which it radically simplifies its action, its duration, its location and the number of its characters. The same is true of the way in which it reduces its meaning to unresolved paradoxes. Finally, as the following section on its structure will suggest, *Waiting for Godot* is also peculiarly Post-Modern in terms of the way it reflects its author's preoccupation with questions of 'shape' and 'form' in addition to questions of meaning.

The structure of *Waiting for Godot*

The action of the play is *cyclic*, in that the events of Act II largely repeat and parallel those of Act I. The two acts of *Waiting for Godot* therefore appear to be parts of an endless series, as Vladimir seems to realise when he comments, 'Off we go again' (p.91). Ihab Hassan points out: 'The inaction of the play is cyclical, and its events are endlessly repetitious; its two acts are symmetric, both equal images of an absence. Two acts, as Samuel Beckett knew, are enough to represent a sequence stretching to infinity.'*

Beckett's 1975 Schiller Theater production of *Waiting for Godot* (referred to in Part 2, p.17) emphasised not only the cyclic nature of the play, in the repetitions of language and action, but brought out the visual-aural balance within the contrasting comic routines and the language rhythms of which the play is composed. Words were liberally invaded by silence, while periods of movement were punctuated by stillness. Yet the production went at a tremendous pace. Language rhythms sprang to life, as speeches were rapidly delivered like a comedian's patter, while comic action routines constantly called to mind the circus clown.

Walter Asmus (Beckett's production assistant) remarked that 'In the blocking and in the construction of the dialogues there is a structure of repetitions, variations, similarities, parallels, of echoes and accumulated references, and these are realised in the production as concrete structure and form.'** As the detailed summaries in Part 2 show, Beckett constantly repeats certain similar actions or statements in order

*Ihab Hassan, *The Literature of Silence: Henry Miller and Samuel Beckett*, Peter Smith, New York, 1967, p.176.
**Theatre Quarterly*, Vol. V, no.19 (London, 1975), p.25.

both to give his work a clear structure and to emphasise the monotonous and repetitious nature of reality in the play.

When discussing the play with his actors, Beckett is reported to have stated that it should be performed 'very simply', so as 'to give confusion shape'. According to Beckett, the ideal production should stress:

> A shape through repetition, repetition of themes. Not only themes in the script, but also themes of the body. When at the beginning Estragon is asleep leaning on the stone, that is a theme that repeats itself a few times. There are fixed points of writing, where everything stands completely still, where silence threatens to swallow everything up. Then the action starts again.*

The 1975 production was a further illustration of the theories of dramatic shape and movement that Beckett had formed since his first experience as a director of his plays. Discussing these theories with Charles Marowitz in 1962, Beckett observed:

> Producers don't seem to have any sense of form in movement. The kind of form one finds in music, for instance, where themes keep recurring. When in a text actions are repeated, they ought to be made unusual the first time, so that when they happen again—in exactly the same way—an audience will recognize them from before. In the revival of *Godot* (in Paris) I tried to get at something of that stylized movement that's in the play.**

In sum, *Waiting for Godot* is a typically Post-Modern composition insofar as it not only emphasises questions of shape, structure and stylised movement and diction in order *to create an explicit form*, but also employs such structural devices *to clarify its thematic content*: an ambiguous content which is wonderfully emphasised by the play's carefully balanced components.

The style of *Waiting for Godot*

Waiting for Godot has a number of unusual stylistic features. Perhaps the most striking aspect of the play's style is the way it juxtaposes sequences of extremely brief and simple exchanges with moments of highly elaborate or poetic language. This kind of effect is partially exemplified on the first page of the play. Vladimir's sarcastic use of unusually formal language is followed by an exchange in which he and Estragon both echo and contradict each other's rapid statements.

VLADIMIR: (*hurt, coldly*). May one enquire where His Highness spent the night?

* *Theatre Quarterly*, Vol. V, no.19 (London, 1975), p.23.
** *Encore* (March/April, 1962), p.44.

ESTRAGON: In a ditch.
VLADIMIR: (*admiringly*). A ditch! Where?
ESTRAGON: (*without gesture*). Over there.
VLADIMIR: And they didn't beat you?
ESTRAGON: Beat me? Certainly they beat me.
VLADIMIR: The same lot as usual?
ESTRAGON: The same? I don't know. (p.9)

Nearly every line echoes or contradicts the previous line. Thus we hear: 'a ditch'/'A ditch!'; 'Where?'/'there'; 'beat you?'/'Beat me?'; 'The same'/'The same?'. As with most of the play's dialogues, conversation does not lead anywhere. This dialogue ends inconclusively with the words, 'I don't know.'

Often such exchanges have an extremely formal quality, consisting of four statements of which the last is the same as the second. Typical of this 'one, two, three, two' pattern are the following lines from Act II. In each of these two extracts, extremely formalised sequences of words lead to another unusual stylistic feature of the play: its use of '*Silence*' and '*Long silence*'.

VLADIMIR: Rather they whisper.
ESTRAGON: They rustle.
VLADIMIR: They murmur.
ESTRAGON: They rustle.
        Silence. (p.63)

VLADIMIR: They make a noise like feathers.
ESTRAGON: Like leaves.
VLADIMIR: Like ashes.
ESTRAGON: Like leaves.
        Long silence. (p.63)

Just as Estragon repeats 'rustle' and 'leaves' in the passages above, other statements such as 'Nothing to be done' (pp.9, 11, 21) and 'We're waiting for Godot' (pp.14, 78, 84) are continually echoed word for word, or in variations, throughout the play.

Certain symbolic images and objects (such as Estragon's feet and Vladimir's hat) are also emphasised by means of repetition. Indeed, the repetitious style of the dialogue and the stage directions, and *Waiting for Godot*'s cyclical action, become inseparable aspects of what Walter Asmus calls the play's 'structure of repetitions' (see notes on *Waiting for Godot*'s structure, pp.45–6).

The main exceptions to this 'structure of repetitions' are the occasional speeches about the true nature of reality, such as Lucky's tirade (pp.42–5), Pozzo's outburst about the brevity of life (p.89) and Vladimir's final speech (pp.90–91). All of these speeches are unusually forceful. Lucky's tirade reveals exceptional incoherence, whereas Pozzo's and Vladimir's speeches contain extremely striking poetic imagery. In all three cases, these speeches are caused by moments of inhabitual thought about the reality of man's condition. In each instance, therefore, the style is naturally very different to the 'habitual' superficial comments of the characters.

The styles of the play, then, seem to consist of three distinct kinds of discourse (or failed discourse):
(i) Sequences of carefully structured, brief exchanges.
(ii) Moments of completely failed discourse, described as 'Silence' or 'Long silence'.
(iii) Rare outbursts of extremely concentrated 'poetic' or 'incoherent' speech.

The peculiarly brief and peculiarly structured 'habitual' exchanges of Vladimir and Estragon are typically Post-Modern in terms of their highly simplified form and content. Beckett's frequent use of highly effective moments of silence may be seen as an extreme consequence of Post-Modernism's simplification of language.

The characters

Waiting for Godot contains seven characters: Godot, Vladimir, Estragon, Pozzo, Lucky, a boy and his brother, the shepherd. With the exception of Godot and the brother of the boy who keeps the goats, each character appears in both acts of the play, at the same place, at the same time, on two successive days.

The difference between these two days is extremely significant. The characters in *Waiting for Godot* are not simply dramatically interesting as characters who react to one another. They are also of interest because of the ways in which they react to the influence of time, be this a question of their ability to distinguish one day from another, a question of their habitual means of passing time, or a question of the way in which they may be transformed from one day to the next by 'chance'.

Godot

Very little is known about Godot. The Boy thinks that he has a white beard (p.92); reports that he 'does nothing' for a living (p.91); and reveals that he does not beat him, although he does beat his brother who 'minds the sheep' (p.51). Vladimir hopes to be 'saved' by Godot (p.94); and while claiming that he and Estragon are not 'tied' to Godot 'for the moment' (p.21), realises that if they ignored Godot 'He'd punish us' (p.93). He also tells Estragon that Godot 'didn't say for sure he'd come' (p.14), and that they requested 'nothing very definite' from him (p.18).

Since Godot never arrives, and very little else is discovered about him, he remains an extremely vague character. Fletcher, Fletcher, Smith and Bachem report Beckett's suggestion that Vladimir despairs on learning that Godot has a white beard (p.92), because this sign of old age indicates that Godot will be too familiar with the fact that there is 'Nothing to be done' to attempt to save Vladimir and Estragon. According to Beckett, 'If he were less experienced there might be some hope.'*

Vladimir

Vladimir is usually described by such stage directions as 'He reflects' (p.9), 'musingly' (p.10), and 'deep in thought' (p.11), and might therefore be said to be a thinker. It is Vladimir who comments, 'What are we doing here, *that* is the question' (p.80), and who ponders, 'Tomorrow, when I wake, or think I do, what shall I say of today? . . . But in all that what truth will there be?' (p.90).

Vladimir is also relatively optimistic. He finds life 'too much for one man', but cheerfully adds, 'On the other hand what's the good of losing heart now' (p.10). He is consoled by the fact that one of the thieves crucified with Christ was saved, finding this 'a reasonable percentage' (p.11). While Estragon argues that life gets progressively 'worse', Vladimir comments, 'With me it's just the opposite . . . I get used to the muck as I go along' (p.21).

It seems that Vladimir once saved Estragon's life, fishing him out of the river Rhône (p.53). His benevolence is again revealed when he seems keen to answer Pozzo's cries for help in Act II (p.79). Vladimir has little sympathy for Estragon's *mental torments*, refusing to hear about them, with the words 'Don't tell me!' (pp.16, 70, 90). Nevertheless, Vladimir sympathises with Estragon's habitual physical discomforts. He 'tenderly' offers to carry Estragon when his leg hurts (p.32), and displays great consideration for the sleeping Estragon when he 'gets up softly, takes off his coat and lays it across Estragon's shoulders' (p.70).

Like Estragon, Vladimir suffers from physical ailments, walking in an agitated manner because of his enlarged prostate gland. A man who thinks and speaks, he is associated with the habit of examining his hat, and with 'stinking breath' (p.46).

Estragon

Estragon was once a poet (p.12), and appears to be a character who feels rather than thinks. Although he tries to find peace by falling asleep, he is constantly 'restored to the horror of his situation' (p.15),

*Fletcher et al., A Student's Guide to the Plays of Samuel Beckett, p.70.

that is, to a state of mental anguish. This anguish takes the form of his nightmares (pp.16, 70); or else seems to take the form of painful moments when he realises that he is 'unhappy' (p.50), 'accursed' (p.73) and 'in hell!' (p.74).

As a result of such moments of anguish, Estragon finds that life gets increasingly worse (p.21). He complains about his 'lousy life' (p.61) and about his 'puke of a life' (p.62), causing Vladimir to comment, 'I've had about my bellyful of your lamentations!' (p.71).

Although Estragon echoes the poet Shelley (p.52), and invents the insult 'Crritic!' (p.75), he often experiences great difficulty in expressing himself in words. Sometimes he uses gestures instead of words, referring to himself with a 'gesture towards his rags' (p.12), and referring to the world in general with a 'gesture towards the universe' (p.16). Towards the end of the play, Estragon finds he cannot communicate his feelings in either words or gestures, and simply offers 'wild gestures, incoherent words' (p.89).

Like Vladimir, Estragon suffers from physical ailments. One of his feet always hurts (pp.10 and 48) and one of his lungs is weak (p.40). As a 'physical' man who prefers sleep to speech and thought, he is associated with his painful boots and with 'stinking feet' (p.46).

Pozzo

According to Deirdre Bair, both Beckett and Roger Blin (the first director of *Waiting for Godot*) saw Pozzo 'as an English gentleman farmer, carrying a case of wine bottles, wearing . . . a beautiful necktie, bowler hat and gleaming leather riding boots'.* Mary Benson also quotes Blin as saying that Beckett had imagined Pozzo 'as a kind of mass, of flesh', with 'a "fat" voice'.** Briefly, Pozzo seems to be a very commanding figure, both in terms of his social position and in terms of his physical stature.

Pozzo's commanding nature is exemplified by his first utterances: the orders 'On!', 'Back!' and 'Be careful!' (p.22). Spoken in a 'terrifying voice', his first communication to Vladimir and Estragon is the proud assertion, 'I am Pozzo!' (p.22).

While Vladimir and Estragon are trapped in an unchanging, cyclical relationship, Pozzo seems to illustrate the fall of a proud, assertive possessor. At the beginning of the play Pozzo emphasises that he is a landowner, telling Vladimir and Estragon that they are 'on my land' (p.23). He also reveals that he owns Lucky, whom he is about to sell at a fair (p.32), plus a quantity of baggage. As the play progresses he loses

*Deirdre Bair, *Samuel Beckett*, p.422.
**Mary Benson, 'Roger Blin and Beckett', *London Magazine*, Vol. 18, no.7 (October 1978), pp.52–7, 55.

such minor possessions as his pipe (p.34), his pulveriser (p.40) and his watch (p.46); and by the end of the play he has become a helpless blind man, having also lost his sight.

Pozzo remarks that he owes his early fortune not so much to personal qualities as to *chance*. Speaking with reference to his slave, Lucky, he observes, 'Remark that I might just as well have been in his shoes and he in mine. If chance had not willed it otherwise' (p.31). His sudden blindness seems similarly due to chance, and Pozzo emphasises the arbitrary quality of chance (or fate or fortune) by describing himself as being 'as blind as Fortune' (p.86). Notice that Vladimir also considers himself to be controlled by 'a cruel fate' (p.79).

Elsewhere, while discussing the change from day to night, Pozzo seems to characterise the surprising way in which 'chance' reverses his own condition later in the play. He remarks that 'Night . . . will burst upon us (*snaps his fingers*) pop! like that! . . . just when we least expect it', concluding, 'That's how it is on this bitch of an earth' (p.38). One of Pozzo's characteristics is therefore to illustrate the *general principle* that man's condition, and changes in man's condition, are to a large extent the consequence of *chance* rather than of man's *decisions and actions*.

Pozzo's comments to Vladimir and Estragon exemplify man's need for human companionship. Pozzo admits he 'cannot go for long without the society of my likes' (p.24); confesses, 'I don't like talking in a vacuum' (p.30); and encourages Vladimir and Estragon to comment on his speeches, since he has 'such need of encouragement' (p.38).

At the same time, Pozzo's relationship with Lucky also seems to suggest that most close relationships are complicated mixtures of love, hatred and dependence. On one occasion Pozzo confides that Lucky 'used to be so kind . . . and now . . . he's killing me' (p.34). But at other times he shows little concern for Lucky. Addressing Lucky as 'pig' and 'hog' (p.23), Pozzo cruelly urges Estragon to 'give him a taste of his boot, in the face and the privates as far as possible' (p.87). Paradoxically, although Pozzo *plans* to sell Lucky, he never gets rid of him. This is probably because Pozzo needs Lucky to carry his baggage and to carry out his orders (just as Lucky seems to depend on Pozzo to give him orders). Finally, Pozzo is literally tied to Lucky, depending upon Lucky's sight to guide him on his way.

At times Pozzo, like Estragon and Vladimir, has difficulty expressing himself, making such statements as, 'Perhaps I haven't got it quite right. He wants to mollify me, so that I'll give up the idea of parting with him. No, that's not exactly it either' (p.31). Despite such difficulties, Pozzo makes several general statements, such as his comment concerning the rapidity with which night falls (p.38), in what has been called his '"impersonal" voice'.* The most important of these general-

*Fletcher *et al.*, *A Student's Guide to the Plays of Samuel Beckett*, p.40.

52 · Commentary

isations is his speech about the brevity of life, which only 'gleams an instant' (p.89).

Lucky

Lucky's first utterance is 'a terrible cry' (p.21). Once on stage, Lucky assumes the attitude of 'one sleeping on his feet'. The stage directions specify: 'Lucky sags slowly, until bag and basket touch the ground, then straightens up with a start and begins to sag again' (p.25). In other words, Lucky is characterised by a cyclical routine in which he is forever 'sagging' and then 'straightening up'. He seems to be on the point of dying, but as the following exchange between Estragon and Vladimir suggests, Lucky's precise condition—like that of almost everything in the play—is difficult to define.

ESTRAGON: Looks at his last gasp to me.
VLADIMIR: It's not certain. (p.26)

According to Deirdre Bair, 'Beckett envisioned Lucky as a porter, with the short gray jacket and black cap worn by workers in Paris railway stations'.* Beckett is reported by Colin Duckworth to have explained Lucky's name with the comment, 'I suppose he is Lucky to have no more expectations',** and it certainly seems true that Lucky expects very little. At most, he simply awaits Pozzo's orders and kicks strangers (p.32).

Pozzo claims that Lucky taught him about beauty, grace and truth (p.33), and also claims that Lucky was once kind but is now 'killing' him (p.34), but the play offers little evidence to substantiate these statements. Pozzo also claims that Lucky 'used to dance . . . For joy', but now Lucky only dances 'The Net': the dance of someone who 'thinks he's entangled in a net' (p.40). Lucky is literally 'entangled' insofar as he is tied by a rope to Pozzo. Pozzo remarks that Lucky once refused to dance (p.40), but this incident is never explained.

Unlike Pozzo, who is totally bald (p.33), and who seems to be more of an 'eater' than a 'thinker', Lucky has long white hair (p.33), and is capable of thinking once his hat is on his head. Lucky's incoherent 'tirade' (pp.42–5) not only exemplifies the difficulties that all the characters experience when attempting to express themselves verbally, but also presents three of the play's central themes. These are: the indifference of heaven ('divine apathia'); the dwindling of man ('man . . . is seen to waste and pine'); and the 'cold' quality of existence ('the earth abode of stones'). (See Part 2, pp.24–6.)

*Deirdre Bair, *Samuel Beckett*, p.421.
**Colin Duckworth, 'The Making of Godot' in Casebook on *Waiting for Godot*, ed. Ruby Cohn, Grove Press, New York, 1967, p.95.

Like Pozzo, Lucky is the victim of a sudden change, becoming dumb (p.89). Just as Pozzo is forever 'tied' by his dependence upon Lucky, Lucky seems permanently 'tied' to Pozzo.

The Boy and his brother, the shepherd

Almost nothing is known of these two characters, save that Godot beats the shepherd but not his brother who keeps the goats. Like Estragon (p.48) and Pozzo (p.88), the Boy has a bad memory, and cannot remember meeting Vladimir (p.91). Just as Pozzo becomes blind and Lucky becomes dumb, the Boy's brother is reported to be 'sick' in Act II (p.92), confirming Lucky's observation that man is doomed to 'waste and pine' (p.43).

Vladimir and Estragon: similarities and contradictions

In order to discover the primary concerns of *Waiting for Godot*, it is necessary to consider Vladimir and Estragon, the two main characters, as a couple. Unlike Pozzo and Lucky, who suffer radical physical changes (becoming blind and dumb by chance), Vladimir and Estragon's condition remains more or less the same.

Nevertheless, despite their fundamental differences (such as the contrast between Vladimir's optimism and Estragon's pessimism), they frequently use exactly the same phrases when describing their general condition. They both find that there is 'Nothing to be done' at the beginning of the play (pp.9 and 11). They both describe their physical complaints with the expression, 'Hurt! He wants to know if it hurts!' (p.10). Finally, at the end of the play, they both remark, 'I can't go on' (pp.91 and 94).

The differences and the similarities between Vladimir's and Estragon's words, gestures and feelings are very significant.

(i) First, such differences reveal the typically Post-Modern doubts that Beckett seems to entertain regarding man's ability to understand or explain his condition. Vladimir and Estragon frequently confuse words, such as 'Godot', 'Pozzo' and 'Bozzo' (p.22) and 'on' and 'off' (p.94). They also continually contradict each other's definitions by using such contrasting terms as 'bush' and 'shrub' (p.14) or 'turnip' and 'carrot' (p.20). Vladimir finds such contradictions very annoying, and complains to Estragon that 'Nothing is certain when you're about' (p.14).

(ii) Secondly, such contradictions offer Vladimir and Estragon a partial advantage, since they provide a painless means of passing the time. In order to avoid being surprised by sudden moments of anguish in which they are 'restored to the horror of their situation', and which they associate with 'the danger . . . of thinking' in an *inhabitual* way (p.64), they prefer to pass their time 'blathering about nothing in particular' (p.66). Estragon frequently suggests various habitual ways in which they can play with language, saying, 'let's ask each other questions' (p.64); 'Let's abuse each other' (p.75); and 'Let's contradict each other' (p.64). As a result, many of their conversations merely list successive contradictory terms, such as 'wings', 'leaves' and 'sand' (p.62) or 'occupation', 'relaxation' and 'recreation' (p.69).

(iii) A third category of contradictions consists of Vladimir's and Estragon's comments upon the play's action. A distinctive 'self-reflective' comedy results from such exchanges as:

VLADIMIR: This is becoming really insignificant.
ESTRAGON: Not enough. (p.68)

and as:

ESTRAGON: It's awful.
VLADIMIR: Worse than the pantomime.
ESTRAGON: The circus.
VLADIMIR: The music-hall. (p.35)

(iv) A fourth form of contradiction occurs when characters question their own judgements and reactions. Such questions seem to exemplify certain general problems. Thus the general fear that all life may be nothing more than a dream is expressed by Vladimir when he asks, 'Was I sleeping, while the others suffered? Am I sleeping now?' (p.90); and by Pozzo, when he similarly ponders, 'Sometimes I wonder if I'm not still asleep' (p.86).

(v) A fifth and final consequence of Vladimir's and Estragon's verbal contradictions and general failure to communicate with words is their attempt to communicate without words by using gestures. As has been observed, Estragon sometimes uses gestures instead of words (pp.12, 16). But the most memorable gestures that Vladimir and Estragon use seem to be those with which they express affection. Even though they frequently declare their wish to leave one another, and even though Estragon claims he only wishes to *be* with Vladimir, and rejects Vladimir's words and gestures, pleading, 'Don't touch me! Don't question me! Don't speak to me! Stay with me!' (p.58), they often express great affection for one another with gestures. Typical of this is the way that Vladimir places his coat on the sleeping Estragon (p.70), and their occasional pauses to embrace in silence (pp.17, 58, 76). According to Roger Blin, these gestures somehow counterbalance the play's pessimism so that

'One is left with a feeling of tenderness.'* This tenderness is probably made more explicit by actors on the stage, rather than by the
printed text of the play.

To conclude these observations, it seems that if the couple composed of
Pozzo and Lucky demonstrates that:
  (i) man's condition is determined by chance;
  (ii) man's condition inevitably gets worse,
the couple formed by Vladimir and Estragon illustrates:
  (i)   the inevitable contradictions that occur when two people try to
        define the same reality;
  (ii) the fact that time can be passed fairly painlessly when two people
        play with language in a habitual way so as to avoid inhabitual
        perceptions of their true condition;
  (iii) the boredom of habitual life (and of the 'action' in *Waiting for
        Godot*);
  (iv) the fact that an individual can often contradict himself, and
        question his own judgements;
  (v)   man's capacity to express affection successfully by using gestures
        rather than words.

The general vision of *Waiting for Godot*

Beckett has stipulated that the keyword in his plays is 'perhaps'.** It
has also been suggested that the carefully balanced structure of *Waiting
for Godot* emphasises the thematic ambiguity created by the play's
contradictory couples of characters.

   The play's vision could be seen as a mixture of optimism and pessimism: the kind of mixture that Vladimir contemplates when reflecting
that of the two thieves crucified with Christ 'One . . . was saved' (p.11).
Moreover, Beckett has often referred to St Augustine's meditation on
this incident—the meditation, 'Do not despair; one of the thieves was
saved. Do not presume; one of the thieves was damned.'† Critics such
as Ruby Cohn have argued that the various couples in *Waiting for
Godot*—Vladimir and Estragon; Pozzo and Lucky; the Boy and his
brother, the shepherd—are all in similar situations to the two thieves
mentioned by Vladimir and by St Augustine.††

   But is this really the case? Vladimir and St Augustine both refer to a

---

*Roger Blin, quoted by Mary Benson in 'Roger Blin and Beckett', *London Magazine*,
Vol. 18, no.7 (October 1978), p.57.
**Quoted by Tom F. Driver in 'Beckett by the Madeleine', *Columbia University Forum*
(Summer 1961), p.23.
†Deirdre Bair, *Samuel Beckett*, p.386.
††Ruby Cohn, 'Beckett's German *Godot*', *Journal of Beckett Studies*, no.1 (Winter
1976), pp.41–9, 43.

situation in which one of two people is saved. There are indeed three couples in *Waiting for Godot*, but not one character in the play can definitely be said to have been saved. Not one character's condition can be said to have improved. But several characters find their circumstances have declined: Pozzo becoming blind; Lucky becoming dumb; and the shepherd brother becoming sick. The only chance of salvation seems to depend upon the arrival of Godot. Godot never arrives.

At best, the characters show gestures of tenderness to one another. At worst, they are extremely cruel to one another. Usually they are distressed, and their most common utterance is 'Help!' (a cry uttered by Estragon (p.10), by Vladimir (p.63) and by Pozzo (p.77)). Estragon's most desperate cry, uttered 'at the top of his voice', is 'God have pity on me!' (p.77). But no sign of divine pity is ever manifested in the play.

According to all the evidence of the play, none of the characters is ever going to be saved, though it seems likely that Pozzo and Lucky will suffer further afflictions. If the play does *not* seem utterly pessimistic, this is probably for four main reasons:

(i)   Firstly, there is a great deal of verbal and gestural comedy in the play, and this comedy seems to lessen the 'horror' of the characters' situation.

(ii) Secondly, the play's explicitly balanced structure offers a certain aesthetic satisfaction which lessens the impact of the play's pessimistic implications.

(iii) Thirdly, the play contains a number of movingly tender gestures which seem to compensate for moments of extreme cruelty.

(iv) Fourthly, and most significantly, the play does not definitely end. The two acts seem to be parts of an endless series. Consequently the play's action remains open-ended, moving towards a 'tomorrow' when Godot may perhaps arrive.

The reader must decide whether or not the reasons above are convincing. Most of the time the general vision of *Waiting for Godot* seems very pessimistic. But, as Estragon observes, 'It's not certain' (p.53).

The achievement of *Waiting for Godot*

Beckett is reported to have found *Waiting for Godot* to be a 'bad play', and is said to consider his novels to be his most significant work.* Nevertheless, Beckett's novels are very difficult to read. It therefore seems that *Waiting for Godot* is most important as a play which has made Beckett's ideas, and his literary genius, accessible to a worldwide public.

The attraction of this play seems to reside in its universality: it is a play that can be interpreted by any number of readers or spectators in

*Quoted by Deirdre Bair in *Samuel Beckett*, p.388.

any number of ways. This universality results from its simplicity and its generality. It is certainly possible to relate the play to precise historical events, such as the condition of France during the Second World War;* to precise religious doctrines, such as Christianity;** to precise philosophical systems, such as those of Heidegger, Hegel, or Sartre;† or to the circumstances of Beckett's private life.††

The attraction and the achievement of *Waiting for Godot*, however, lie not so much in the fact that the play serves any one of these ends, as in the fact that the play is *open-ended*. Several statements by Beckett help to define this achievement. Beckett has insisted that *Waiting for Godot* is a play that is 'striving all the time to avoid definition'.‡ He also emphasises that the play's indefinable quality results from its simplicity. Beckett's letters contain such comments as, 'Why do people have to complicate a thing so simple!'‡‡ and 'I feel the only line is . . . to insist on the extreme simplicity of dramatic situation and issue . . . we have no elucidations to offer.'§

It would be possible to blame Beckett's play for failing to offer any answers, and for merely asking questions. But the fact remains that as an ambiguous and haunting structure, *Waiting for Godot* is a remarkable achievement. Even those critics who regret the absence of any clear moral message in the play would probably share the conclusions of William Empson, who wrote: 'I would hate to suggest a moral censorship against the play; it is so well done that it is an enlarging experience, very different for different members of the audience.'§§

---

*Kay Boyle, 'All Mankind is Us', in *Samuel Beckett, A Collection of criticism*, ed. Ruby Cohn, McGraw-Hill, New York, 1975, pp.15–19.
**G.S. Fraser, 'They Also Serve', *Times Literary Supplement*, (10 February 1956), p.84.
†Günther Anders, 'Being without Time': On Beckett's Play *Waiting for Godot*, in *Samuel Beckett, A Collection of Critical Essays*, ed. Martin Esslin, Prentice-Hall, Englewood Cliffs, New Jersey, 1965, pp.140–51.
††Deirdre Bair, *Samuel Beckett*, p.385.
‡Quoted by Deirdre Bair in *Samuel Beckett*, p.385.
‡‡Quoted by Deirdre Bair in *Samuel Beckett*, p.453.
§Quoted by Deirdre Bair in *Samuel Beckett*, p.470.
§§William Empson in 'Letters to the Editor', *Times Literary Supplement* (30 March 1958), p.195.

Part 4

Hints for study

Waiting for Godot can be studied closely in terms of two main topics: the major themes of the play and the major incidents of the play.

The major themes

Waiting for Godot is a play characterised by balanced form and ambiguous content. It is therefore not surprising to find that most of the major themes consist of dual possibilities, one positive and one negative. These themes appear to fall into five clusters, concerning: Godot; the friendship of Vladimir and Estragon; the problem of the individual's perceptions; the problem of the individual's actions; and the general condition of the universe.

Godot

The themes associated with Godot are all concerned with the uncertainty of his actions and decisions.

Godot may save Vladimir and Estragon (p.94) *or* he may punish them (p.93).

Vladimir and Estragon may be free for the moment (p.21) *or* they may be tied to Godot (p.20).

Godot may treat his servants kindly (p.51) *or* he may beat them (p.51).

The friendship of Vladimir and Estragon

The themes associated with Vladimir and Estragon are all concerned with the uncertain quality of their friendship.

They may be pleased to see one another (p.9) *or* they may wish to part (p.16).

They may sometimes both desire to embrace (p.76) *or* one of them may refuse to be touched by the other (p.58).

They may wish to talk to each other (p.64) *or* one may refuse to listen to the other (p.16).

The problem of the individual's perceptions

The themes associated with the individual's perceptions are all concerned with the uncertainty of all knowledge.

The individual may be awake, perceiving the truth (p.90) *or* he may be asleep (p.91).

The individual may remember things (p.61) *or* he may forget all about them (p.48).

The individual may find that essential reality does not change (p.21) *or* he may find that everything changes (p.60).

The problem of the individual's actions

The themes associated with the individual's actions are all concerned with the uncertain value of any particular action.

The individual may find certain circumstances in which he may do something helpful (p.79) *or* he may conclude that there is nothing to be done (p.9).

The individual may protest when he sees instances of cruelty (p.27) *or* he may abandon all his rights (p.19).

The individual may wait in hope of salvation (p.94) *or* may plan to kill himself (p.17).

The general condition of the universe

The themes concerned with the universe are all concerned with the uncertain quality of existence.

The universe may be ordered by a God with pity for his creations (p.77) *or* the universe might be controlled by chance or a cruel fate (p.79).

The universe may sometimes seem peaceful (p.38) *or* it may be conditioned by sudden changes (p.38).

The quantity of sorrow in the universe may be constant, so that man's condition is not really getting worse (p.33) *or* man may continually be seen to waste and pine, finding that his condition is forever getting worse (p.43).

The major incidents

The major incidents in *Waiting for Godot* can be subdivided into *habitual* and *inhabitual* categories. Habitual incidents are characterised by their symmetrical structure, and usually serve to illustrate the cyclical quality of existence and to offer amusing forms of repetitious action. Inhabitual actions are characterised by their unusual intensity. Usually they take the form of passionate speeches summarising the main themes of the play.

The following fourteen incidents should be examined carefully, in terms of both their form and their content. The first seven incidents exemplify 'habitual action' in *Waiting for Godot*:

(a) **The opening dialogue (p.9):** An introduction to some of the main themes, and to Vladimir's and Estragon's habitual way of exchanging simple comments which echo, vary and contradict each other.

(b) **The end of Act I (pp.53–4):** A striking illustration of the way in which Vladimir and Estragon are tied both to themselves and to Godot. They wonder if they would not be better off alone, and finally plan to leave the country road, but remain there together.

(c) **Vladimir's song (pp.57–8):** Notice how the structure of this song illustrates the cyclical vision of the play.

(d) **Vladimir's and Estragon's dialogue (p.63):** An example of the way in which Vladimir and Estragon use carefully structured dialogues to pass the time. Notice the anguish that Vladimir suffers when confronted by a long silence in which he may begin to think about the reality of his condition.

(e) **The clowning with the hats (pp.71–2):** An example of the way in which Beckett employs the comedy of repetitious *gestures*.

(f) **The multiple fall of Pozzo, Lucky, Vladimir and Estragon (pp.81–2):** Another example of Beckett's use of comic gestures. Notice that Beckett has also described this fall as 'the visual expression of their common situation'.*

(g) **The end of Act II (pp.91–4):** Notice that the dialogue with the Boy, and Vladimir's and Estragon's final inconclusive decision to go, both exemplify their issueless predicament. Compare the end of Act II with the end of Act I.

The following seven incidents exemplify 'inhabitual action':

(h) **Estragon's nightmare (pp.15–16):** Vladimir's refusal to listen to Estragon's nightmare not only exemplifies his unwillingness to contemplate inhabitual reality, but also prompts Estragon's comment: 'This one is enough for you?' This is one of the first of several references to the characters' feeling that they are already suffering '*enough*'.

(i) **Pozzo's speech on tears (p.33):** Pozzo's speech presents the theory that there is a *constant* quantity of sorrow, and that Estragon's sudden pain 'replaces' Lucky's sorrow. Notice that by the end of the play the decline of Pozzo and Lucky suggests that the world contains an *ever increasing* quantity of sorrow.

(j) **Lucky's tirade (pp.42–5):** This unusual example of intense thought has several functions. It presents some of the play's main themes; it demonstrates the difficulty that the play's characters experience when attempting to express themselves with language; and it also provides a bizarre form of comedy.

*Quoted by Fletcher *et al.*, *A Student's Guide to the Plays of Samuel Beckett*, p.68.

(k) Vladimir's and Estragon's discussion of the leaves (p.63): Although the main part of Vladimir's and Estragon's discussion of the leaves is 'habitual' in quality, the dialogue from Vladimir's question, 'What do they say?', to Estragon's remark, 'It is not sufficient,' exemplifies the fate of the two speakers. Like the leaves, they find that to have lived is 'not enough' for them: they sometimes 'have to talk about it'. Notice that they prefer to spend their time 'blathering about nothing in particular' (p.66), rather than discussing their real condition. Nevertheless, as the following three incidents demonstrate, the characters in *Waiting for Godot* do occasionally describe their dilemma.

(l) Vladimir's discussion of action (pp.79–80): In this speech, Vladimir rejects 'idle discourse' and discusses the following: the ideal of doing something; the fact that he and Estragon represent 'all mankind'; the suggestion that they are the victims of a 'cruel fate'; and the fact that they inhabit an 'immense confusion'. This plan to act decisively gradually seems to be forgotten as Vladimir recalls that he and Estragon are waiting for Godot.

(m) Pozzo's final speech (p.89): In this speech, Pozzo argues that there is no point in discussing time, and he emphasises the brevity of existence by associating birth with the grave. Note that Vladimir echoes this imagery later (p.90).

Pozzo argues that the notion of *one day* is 'enough', since man can undergo the greatest changes from one day to another. This speech seems to echo his earlier comment upon the sudden way in which night falls (p.38), and also echoes Vladimir's and Estragon's comments upon the way in which a tree can change in a single night (p.66).

Pozzo's use of the word 'enough' seems to be very significant. We have observed that Estragon suggests that one universe is 'enough' (p.16), and that Vladimir and Estragon explain that the leaves talk because it is not 'enough' to have simply lived (p.63). Taken together, these comments using the word 'enough' illustrate the dilemma of *Waiting for Godot*'s characters. They feel they have lived, spoken, thought and suffered 'enough', and yet they cannot stop themselves from continuing to live, speak, think and suffer.

(n) Vladimir's last long speech (pp.90–1): Instead of using 'idle discourse' to pass the time, Vladimir asks a number of revealing questions about his true condition. Is he asleep or awake? Will he remember anything the next day? If he does remember anything, will any of his memories contain the truth? Echoing the 'grave' and 'birth' imagery used by Pozzo, Vladimir reflects that 'habit' helps to deaden his inhabitual perceptions. He imagines that he is asleep and that someone is looking at him, just as he is looking at the sleeping Estragon. Finally he concludes, 'I can't go on', and then questions everything he has stated, asking, 'What have I said?'

Moving from profound questions to pessimistic images of the brevity of life, Vladimir's reflections upon inhabitual aspects of existence lose their intensity as he recollects that habitual actions deaden the pain of consciousness. Feeling confused, Vladimir wonders if he is not asleep, and finally asks himself what he has said.

Briefly, this speech seems to exemplify all the main sensations in *Waiting for Godot*. These are:

(i) moments of *profound self-doubt* (such as, 'Am I sleeping now?');
(ii) moments of *profound despair* (such as, 'I can't go on.');
(iii) moments of *relative comfort caused by habitual actions* (such as the reflection, 'But habit is a great deadener.').

It should be obvious that the most important inhabitual incidents are Pozzo's and Vladimir's final speeches at the end of Act II. Both of these complicated speeches employ many of the play's major themes and images, and should be examined very carefully.

The selection and use of quotations

You should illustrate all comments about *Waiting for Godot* with appropriate quotations. These need not be very long. But all quotations should be discussed in a clear context. Remember to explain why you find that the text you are quoting is important. Brief quotations illustrating the style and aspects of the characters in *Waiting for Godot* are used extensively in the Commentary in Part 3.

The following quotations all refer to central issues in the play. Try to explain the ways in which these quotations can be used to illustrate such issues.

'One of the thieves was saved.' (p.11)
'One daren't laugh any more.' (p.11)
'People are bloody ignorant apes.' (p.13)
'The essential doesn't change.' (p.21)
'I might just as well have been in his shoes.' (p.31)
'The tears of the world are a constant quantity.' (p.33)
'Forget all I said . . . there wasn't a word of truth in it.' (p.34)
'It's awful.' (p.35)
'Behind this veil of gentleness and peace night is charging . . . and will burst upon us . . . pop! like that! . . . just when we least expect it.' (p.38)
'One knows what to expect.' (p.38)
'I have such need of encouragement!' (p.38)
'They all change. Only we can't.' (p.48)
'You don't know if you are unhappy or not?' (p.51)
'Tomorrow everything will be better.' (p.52)

'No, nothing is certain.' (p.53)
'Things have changed here since yesterday.' (p.60)
'We are incapable of keeping silent.' (p.62)
'I don't know why I don't know!' (p.67)
'This is becoming really insignificant.' (p.68)
'Don't tell me!' (p.70)
'There's nothing to do.' (p.74)
'Let us do something.' (p.79)
'What are we doing here, *that* is the question.' (p.80)
'Habit is a great deadener.' (p.91)
'Everything's dead but the tree.' (p.93)
'*They do not move.*' (p.94)

How to arrange your material

Waiting for Godot is a very ambiguous play. Consequently, almost every question about aspects of the play's meaning will require two things: first, the examination of several different interpretations; secondly, the discussion of both positive and negative aspects of the play's vision.

Every essay should fall into three main parts. First, there should be an introduction. Your introduction should explain what you consider the question is asking. It should then introduce the way in which you intend to answer the question, suggesting what your conclusion might be. Your introduction should also indicate the order in which you intend to discuss the different problems raised by the question.

Secondly, your essay should have a middle. This middle part should discuss different problems raised by the question, in the order indicated in your introduction. Discuss each problem in a separate paragraph. Try to illustrate your paragraphs with brief quotations from the text of the play. Memorise suitable quotations for the examination.

Thirdly, your essay will need a conclusion. This should summarise the points made in the middle of the essay. It should explain what these points all imply when considered together, and it should present your final conclusion to the problems described in your introduction. Make sure that your conclusion offers an answer to the question.

Specimen questions

(1) How important is the structure of *Waiting for Godot*?
(2) Does *Waiting for Godot* suggest there is 'Nothing to be done'?
(3) Discuss the roles of Vladimir and Estragon.
(4) Analyse the roles of Pozzo and Lucky.
(5) In what ways is *Waiting for Godot* 'simple' and 'universal'?

(6) Is *Waiting for Godot* a comic play or a pessimistic play?

(7) Is anything certain in *Waiting for Godot*?

(8) Discuss Godot's role in *Waiting for Godot*.

(9) Discuss the ways in which Beckett uses symbols such as the tree, Vladimir's hat, Estragon's feet, Lucky's hair and Pozzo's bald head.

(10) In what ways do the characters of *Waiting for Godot* use language, and in what ways do they find that words 'fail'?

(11) What is the significance of Vladimir's reference to the thief who was 'saved'?

(12) *Waiting for Godot* refers to God, to chance and to fate. What forces seem to dominate the play?

(13) Does life get better or worse in *Waiting for Godot*, or does it simply remain the same?

(14) Why should one differentiate between the two days represented by Act I and Act II?

(15) In what ways is the fate of Pozzo and Lucky different to that of Vladimir and Estragon?

(16) Discuss the ways in which *Waiting for Godot* is a play concerned with either *memory* or *time*.

Specimen answers

How important is the structure of *Waiting for Godot*?

The structure of *Waiting for Godot* is significant for three main reasons. First, it offers the formal satisfaction of a work which can be seen to be a carefully ordered, balanced composition. Secondly, this balanced structure helps to emphasise the themes of the play. Thirdly, the play's balanced structure creates a number of comic effects. This essay will first discuss the formal qualities of *Waiting for Godot*, and will then discuss the ways in which aspects of the play's structure emphasise the themes of *Waiting for Godot*, and create various comic effects.

The most obvious structural quality of the play is that it is composed of two carefully balanced acts. The plot of each act has much in common. In both cases the two main characters, Vladimir and Estragon, meet at the end of the day on a country road to wait together for Godot. In each act they are surprised by the appearance of Pozzo and his servant Lucky. Finally, in each act a boy visits them after the departure of Pozzo and Lucky, to inform them that Godot will not come on this evening, but is sure to come the following evening. Vladimir comments upon the way in which Act II echoes Act I, remarking, 'Off we go again' (p.91).*

*Page references are given in the model answers for the convenience of readers of these Notes. Obviously there is no need to give page references in examination answers.

The two acts of *Waiting for Godot* are not only balanced in terms of their action, but also in terms of their dialogue. Characters continually echo each other's words by repeating such phrases as 'Nothing to be done', 'I can't go on' and 'We're waiting for Godot'. Perhaps the most striking example of this balanced structure is the end of each act, in which Vladimir and Estragon remark, 'Well, shall we go?' and 'Yes, let's go', but do not move. Together, the balanced structure of the action and the dialogue in the two acts of *Waiting for Godot* give the play a pleasing formal symmetry.

This formal symmetry also emphasises the main themes of the play. *Waiting for Godot* is a play about the repetitious nature of existence, and this central theme is well illustrated by the fact that the endings of the play's two acts are almost identical. Another of the play's themes concerns the way in which chance suddenly alters man's condition. This theme is clearly depicted in terms of the contrasts between the two acts. Vladimir and Estragon notice that the tree, which was previously bare, has become covered with leaves 'in a single night' (p.66). Similarly, Pozzo becomes blind 'all of a sudden' (p.86), and Lucky equally rapidly becomes dumb. *Waiting for Godot* is also a play concerned with the limitations of man's memory. This theme is similarly exemplified by the play's two-act structure. In Act II, after just one night, Estragon can no longer remember having met Pozzo and Lucky in Act I.

A third way in which the structure of *Waiting for Godot* functions is as a source of comedy. Vladimir's repetitive song at the beginning of Act II has an amusing circular structure. Much of Vladimir's and Estragon's conversation is equally carefully composed. Frequently they exchange balanced sequences of short statements, such as the following lines:

ESTRAGON: I am happy.
VLADIMIR: So am I.
ESTRAGON: So am I.
VLADIMIR: We are happy.
ESTRAGON: We are happy. (p.60)

In addition to such amusingly structured conversations, *Waiting for Godot* also contains several sequences of amusingly repetitive gestures, such as Vladimir's habit of examining his hat and Estragon's habit of examining his boot. Another example of carefully structured gestures is the amusing scene in which Vladimir and Estragon repeatedly exchange hats in Act II.

In conclusion, it is clear that the structure of *Waiting for Godot* is significant for three reasons. First, the balanced action and dialogue in the two acts create a very satisfying formal pattern. Secondly, this balanced structure helps to emphasise such themes as the repetitious nature of existence; the way in which chance suddenly alters man's condition; and the limits of man's memory. Thirdly, the structure of individual sequences of dialogue and of gesture provides much of the comic material in the play. Without this carefully balanced structure, *Waiting for Godot* would be a far less successful work.

Does *Waiting for Godot* suggest that there is 'Nothing to be done'?

The first statement in *Waiting for Godot* is Estragon's pessimistic conclusion that there is 'Nothing to be done.' Although this statement may appear to present the theme of the play, *Waiting for Godot*'s message is not simply pessimistic. Much of the play suggests that there is nothing to be done, but the play also at times suggests that something may be done. At other times the play seems extremely ambiguous, and its characters seem very uncertain what to do. This essay will first discuss those parts of the play which suggest that nothing can be done. It will then examine the parts of the play which suggest that something can be done, and finally it will discuss those parts of the play that seem completely ambiguous.

One of the clearest suggestions that there is 'Nothing to be done' in *Waiting for Godot* is voiced in Lucky's tirade in Act I. Here Lucky observes that man's condition cannot improve, since he 'is seen to waste and pine' (p.43). This observation is confirmed by the way in which the condition of several characters in the play becomes dramatically worse in Act II. Lucky himself becomes dumb; Pozzo becomes blind; and the brother of Godot's messenger is reported to have become 'sick' (p.92).

The condition of Vladimir and Estragon does not seem to get worse, but both of them repeatedly insist that they can do nothing worthwhile. They both state 'Nothing to be done' at the beginning of Act I, and both conclude 'I can't go on' at the end of Act II. They both wish to hang themselves; they agree that they should part from each other; and at the end of each act they decide to leave the roadside where they were supposed to wait for Godot. It seems that they cannot even do this, for 'They do not move.' The notion that there is 'Nothing to be done' is thus exemplified both by the decline of Lucky, Pozzo and the Boy's brother, and by the despair and immobility of Vladimir and Estragon.

Paradoxically, in parts of the play Vladimir and Estragon also suggest that certain things can be done. The clearest example of this sentiment is Vladimir's statement, 'Let us do something', in Act II (p.79), when he tries to help the fallen Pozzo. Elsewhere in the play Vladimir and Estragon also help each other in various simple ways. Although Vladimir refuses to listen to accounts of Estragon's nightmares, saying, 'Don't tell me' (p.16), the two friends find ordinary conversation a comforting way of passing the time. Estragon suggests, 'Let's contradict each other' and 'Let's ask each other questions' (p.64). By contradicting each other and by questioning each other, Vladimir and Estragon find that they can *do something* to keep each other from thinking about the reality of their painful condition.

Vladimir and Estragon also comfort one another with gestures, and frequently pause to embrace. One of the most moving moments of the play occurs when Vladimir places his coat over the sleeping Estragon to keep him warm (p.70). Although Vladimir and Estragon often consider parting, they seem to remain together because their words and gestures allow them to do something positive to help each other.

Waiting for Godot thus suggests that there is both nothing to be done and something to be done. It also sometimes simply presents extremely ambiguous circumstances in which it is not clear what should be done. This ambiguity is exemplified by the behaviour of Godot. The play ends with Vladimir and Estragon waiting for Godot, and although Godot has not yet come in either of the two acts of the play, and although the play contains no evidence of any character being saved, it still seems possible that Godot may arrive the following day. The reasons why Vladimir and Estragon are waiting for Godot are themselves very ambiguous: Vladimir only recalls that they asked Godot for 'nothing very definite' (p.18).

Godot's treatment of the two boys who work for him is equally ambiguous. At the end of Act I, the Boy who minds the goats explains that Godot does not beat him, but does beat his brother who minds the sheep. When Vladimir asks him why he is not beaten by Godot, the Boy replies, 'I don't know' (p.51). Vladimir seems equally confused about his own condition. At the end of Act II he exemplifies the bewilderment that all the characters in *Waiting for Godot* feel before their ambiguous condition, by questioning the truth of his own comments with the words, 'What have I said?' (p.91).

In conclusion, it is clear that *Waiting for Godot* does not simply suggest that there is 'nothing to be done'. Rather, the play suggests three distinct points of view. At times it is suggested that there is nothing to be done, because men 'waste and pine', and constantly despair, feeling they 'can't go on'. But at other times the play suggests that something can be done, since men may use words and gestures to comfort their fellow beings. Elsewhere, the play's action remains extremely ambiguous, and its characters seem utterly confused regarding the best thing to do. This ambiguity appears to be characteristic of the entire play, and *Waiting for Godot* is perhaps best considered as Beckett's depiction of the painful confusion and doubt that twentieth-century man experiences when deciding what he should do.

Discuss the roles of Vladimir and Estragon in *Waiting for Godot.*

Vladimir and Estragon have complex roles in *Waiting for Godot.* They not only need to be considered as two of the main individuals in this very ambiguous play, but should also be considered as a couple. This essay will first examine them as individuals. It will then examine a number of ways in which Vladimir and Estragon are significant as a couple. It will be suggested that they form a couple which forms a 'universal' symbol; that they depict the limitations and the comic potential of man's efforts to communicate; and that they offer an important alternative to the fate of the couple composed of Pozzo and Lucky.

In many ways, Vladimir and Estragon are two very different individuals. Vladimir is essentially a thinker who is described as 'musing' (p.9), and who makes such statements as 'What are we doing here, *that* is the question' (p.80). He is also an optimist, believing that 'Tomorrow everything will be better' (p.52). Vladimir is associated with thought in terms of his habit of examining his hat, and is associated with speech in terms of his 'stinking breath' (p.46).

Estragon is presented as somebody who feels rather than thinks, and who makes such intuitive statements as 'I'm accursed' (p.73) and 'I'm in hell' (p.74). Estragon is pessimistic, and observes, 'The more you eat the worse it gets' (p.21). He has a physical rather than a mental personality, and is associated with his habit of examining his painful boot, and with his 'stinking feet' (p.46). Estragon and Vladimir are thus clearly two very dissimilar characters. Their differences seem to have the role both of presenting two contrasting yet equally valid attitudes to life, and of introducing the ambiguous vision of the play.

Vladimir and Estragon are the same, insofar as they share identical conclusions about life. They both state that there is 'Nothing to be done', and at the end of the play claim that they 'can't go on'. In this respect they are symbolic of all men. They also have a 'universal' role because their differences are complementary. When seen together as a couple, their 'mental' and 'physical' personalities combine to represent the entirety of man as mind and body. In other words, they have a 'universal' role both in terms of their identical conclusions and in terms of their complementary personalities.

When considered as a couple, Vladimir and Estragon also illustrate the limitations of man's attempts to communicate through language. They constantly contradict one another. Looking at the same tree, Vladimir calls it a 'shrub' while Estragon calls it a 'tree'. Their conversations also suggest that language can be used in a superficial way to pass the time, and in Act II they deliberately play with language in order to avoid thinking about their condition, abusing each other, contradicting each other and asking each other questions. Such exchanges as 'Sewer-rat!', 'Curate!', 'Cretin!', 'Crritic!' not only illustrate this use of language as a pastime, but also provide much of the comedy in the play. Comedy is also provided by certain repetitious and meaningless actions of Vladimir and Estragon, such as the occasion in Act II when they ritualistically exchange hats.

In addition to this comic role, their actions occasionally suggest that gestures may offer the communication that language fails to afford. They constantly reveal their affection for each other by pausing to embrace, and if Vladimir fails to show his tenderness for Estragon in words, he reveals it very movingly when he places his coat on the sleeping Estragon to keep him warm in Act II. When considered together, Vladimir's and Estragon's contradictory, habitual, comic and tender forms of communication combine to suggest that the quality of their relationship is very ambiguous. It is neither wholly successful nor wholly unsuccessful. Like their different attitudes as individuals, their relationship as a couple confirms the ambiguity of the play's vision.

As a couple, Vladimir and Estragon also offer a very interesting contrast to the couple composed of Pozzo and Lucky. While Vladimir and Estragon's situation does not really change from Act I to Act II, Pozzo and Lucky undergo radical changes, becoming blind and dumb respectively. Vladimir and Estragon thus suggest that life remains the same, forever repeating itself, whereas Pozzo and Lucky seem to show that though life may seem calm and peaceful, it is subject to the sudden changes of 'fate' and 'chance'. The paradoxical permanence of Vladimir's and Estragon's condition thus forms yet another aspect of the ambiguity of *Waiting for Godot*.

In conclusion, it would appear that Vladimir and Estragon have a number of roles in *Waiting for Godot*, and that all of these roles serve to reinforce the play's ambiguous vision. As individuals they offer two utterly different attitudes to life, and yet also share the same conclusions, and function as a universal symbol when seen as two complementary figures. As a couple they reveal the ambiguous quality of man's attempt to communicate with language. While presenting various amusing sequences of words and actions, they also suggest that certain gestures provide valuable forms of communication. Finally, as a couple whose circumstances do not change, Vladimir and Estragon evoke an entirely different condition to that of Pozzo and Lucky. Both individuals *and* a couple, and both different *and* the same, Vladimir and Estragon offer memorable examples of the ambiguous condition of twentieth-century man.

Part 5

Suggestions for further reading

The text

BECKETT, SAMUEL: *Waiting for Godot*, Faber, London, 1978. The play is best studied in this revised and unexpurgated English version, the latest reprint edition.

BECKETT, SAMUEL: *En attendant Godot*, edited by Colin Duckworth, Harrap, London, 1977. This contains an excellent critical introduction which should be read carefully by all students of the play.

Biography

BAIR, DEIRDRE: *Samuel Beckett*, Cape, London, 1978. The conclusions and even some of the facts in this biography of Beckett are often questionable, but it contains much valuable information about him.

Criticism

COE, RICHARD N: *Beckett*, Oliver & Boyd, Edinburgh & London, 1964. A valuable compact introduction to Beckett's work.

COHN, RUBY, (ED.): *Casebook on Waiting for Godot*, Grove Press, New York, 1967. A useful introduction to the play.

COHN, RUBY, (ED.): *Samuel Beckett, A Collection of Criticism*, McGraw-Hill, New York, 1975. A collection of various critical studies, including Kay Boyle's 'All Mankind is Us', which interprets the play in terms of Occupied France in the Second World War.

COHN, RUBY: 'Beckett's German *Godot*', *Journal of Beckett Studies*, No. 1, Winter 1976, pp.41–9. An account of Beckett's 1975 Schiller Theater production of *Godot*.

ESSLIN, MARTIN: *The Theatre of the Absurd*, Pelican Books, Harmondsworth, 1977. A useful introduction to the group of contemporary playwrights (including Beckett, Ionesco, Adamov and Genet) that Esslin associates with the 'theatre of the absurd'.

ESSLIN, MARTIN: *Samuel Beckett, A Collection of Critical Essays*, Prentice-Hall, Englewood Cliffs, New Jersey, 1965. A valuable collection of critical essays on Beckett, including Günther Anders's 'Being without Time: On Beckett's Play *Waiting for Godot*', which exemplifies the way in which *Waiting for Godot* can be interpreted with reference to philosophy.

FEDERMAN, RAYMOND AND FLETCHER, JOHN: *Samuel Beckett, His Works and His Critics*, University of California Press, Berkeley, 1970. A detailed description of Beckett's writings and of much of the criticism published about Beckett up to the time of this book's preparation.

FLETCHER, BERYL; FLETCHER, JOHN; SMITH, BARRY; AND BACHEM, WALTER: *A Student's Guide to the Plays of Samuel Beckett*, Faber, London, 1978. A useful collection of brief but very informative introductions to all of Beckett's plays.

GRAVER, LAWRENCE AND FEDERMAN, RAYMOND: *Samuel Beckett, The Critical Heritage*, Routledge & Kegan Paul, London, 1979. A valuable collection of reviews and criticism of Beckett's work, ranging from 1934 to the present day.

The authors of these notes

ROSEMARY POUNTNEY, who trained as an actress before reading English at the University of Oxford, is now a lecturer in English at University College, Dublin. She has contributed to *Modern Drama* (1976), *Journal of Beckett Studies* (1976) and *The Rising Generation* (1979). She has also performed in plays by Beckett, playing Mouth in *Not I* at the Playhouse, Oxford, in 1976 and at the Irish Theatre Festival in Dublin in 1978, where she also played May in *Footfalls*, a role she played again in Oxford in 1980. She is preparing a book on the manuscripts of Beckett's plays.

NICHOLAS ZURBRUGG studied at the University of Neuchâtel, Switzerland; the University of East Anglia, Norwich; and St John's College, Oxford. He is a lecturer in comparative literature at Griffith University, Brisbane. He has contributed to *A Dictionary of Modern Critical Terms* (edited by Roger Fowler); to *Dada Spectrum: The Dialectics of Revolt* (edited by Stephen Foster and Rudolf Kuenzli); and to *Dada, Studies of a Movement* (edited by Richard Sheppard). He is at present writing a comparative study of Beckett and Proust.